ATTACK AND
COUNTERATTACK
IN CHESS

ABOUT THE AUTHOR

Fred Reinfeld, a Master chess player, is a native New Yorker. It was in the city schools and at City College that he began his chess playing. While still in his teens, he became Intercollegiate Champion, and was victorious in the New York State, Manhattan Club, and Marshall Club championship matches, defeating such worthy opponents as Sammy Reshevsky, Reuben Fine, Arnold Denker, and I. A. Horowitz.

Mr. Reinfeld has been one of the editors of *Chess Review* since its start in 1933. He is a prolific writer, with more than fifty chess books to his credit. Seven of these are Everyday Handbooks: *First Book of Chess* (co-authored with I. A. Horowitz), *Improving Your Chess, How to Win Chess Games Quickly, 1001 Ways to Checkmate, Complete Book of Chess Openings, 1001 Chess Sacrifices and Combinations*, and this volume. He has also written two other Everyday Handbooks, *How to Play Checkers* and *How to Build a Coin Collection*.

ATTACK
AND
COUNTERATTACK
IN CHESS

HOW TO PLAN YOUR GAME AND COPE WITH UNEXPECTED SITUATIONS

Combining *Third and Fourth Books
of Chess* (including 35 pages from
Improving Your Chess) and
Two New Chapters

FRED REINFELD

BARNES & NOBLE, INC.   •   NEW YORK
Publishers • Booksellers • Since 1873
Everyday Handbook

CONTENTS

PART I

White's Point of View

PART II

Black's Point of View

CHESS NOTATION

As indicated in the following diagram, all the squares on the chessboard are *numbered* from both sides of the board; White's KR1, for example, is Black's KR8. Each square is also *named* for the piece occupying the file. Below the diagram is a list of the chief abbreviations used in chess notation.

BLACK

QR1 / QR8	QN1 / QN8	QB1 / QB8	Q1 / Q8	K1 / K8	KB1 / KB8	KN1 / KN8	KR1 / KR8
QR2 / QR7	QN2 / QN7	QB2 / QB7	Q2 / Q7	K2 / K7	KB2 / KB7	KN2 / KN7	KR2 / KR7
QR3 / QR6	QN3 / QN6	QB3 / QB6	Q3 / Q6	K3 / K6	KB3 / KB6	KN3 / KN6	KR3 / KR6
QR4 / QR5	QN4 / QN5	QB4 / QB5	Q4 / Q5	K4 / K5	KB4 / KB5	KN4 / KN5	KR4 / KR5
QR5 / QR4	QN5 / QN4	QB5 / QB4	Q5 / Q4	K5 / K4	KB5 / KB4	KN5 / KN4	KR5 / KR4
QR6 / QR3	QN6 / QN3	QB6 / QB3	Q6 / Q3	K6 / K3	KB6 / KB3	KN6 / KN3	KR6 / KR3
QR7 / QR2	QN7 / QN2	QB7 / QB2	Q7 / Q2	K7 / K2	KB7 / KB2	KN7 / KN2	KR7 / KR2
QR8 / QR1	QN8 / QN1	QB8 / QB1	Q8 / Q1	K8 / K1	KB8 / KB1	KN8 / KN1	KR8 / KR1

WHITE

King — K	check — ch		
Queen — Q	discovered check — dis ch		
Rook — R	double check — dbl ch		
Bishop — B	en passant — e.p.		
Knight — N	good move — !		
Pawn — P	very good move — ! !		
captures — x	outstanding move — ! ! !		
to — —	bad move — ?		

Chapter One

HOW TO CONTROL THE CENTER

YOU ARE about to start playing a game of chess. The pieces and Pawns are all set up in their proper opening positions. You are playing White. What is the basic thought that will guide you through the opening during the first few moves?

You know that it is important to bring out your pieces quickly and effectively. You have been told that it is a good idea to begin by moving up one of your center Pawns. You have been advised to control the center.

"Control the center"—that is the basic idea of opening play. But just what is the center? how do you control it? and why is it important to control it?

1

The squares inside the heavy lines make up the center.

The center, as you can see from Diagram 1, is made up of the squares King 3, Queen 3, King Bishop 4, King 4, Queen 4,

Queen Bishop 4, King Bishop 5, King 5, Queen 5, Queen Bishop 5, King 6, Queen 6.

When you post ("centralize") your pieces in the center, they have their greatest range and power. Once you play them to the center during the opening, they can be moved quickly to other sectors as the course of the game requires.

We often use the term "center" in a restricted sense, referring only to the inner four squares: King 4, Queen 4, King 5, and Queen 5. These are the most effective squares for center Pawns. Why? Because a Pawn at King 4 or Queen 4 prevents hostile pieces from establishing themselves at the center squares controlled by that Pawn.

"Controlling the center," then, means *posting your Pawns and pieces in such a way that you have a decidedly more powerful grip on the center than your opponent has.*

White has the first move. Consequently his chance of controlling the center is a pretty good one. Now let us turn to some examples which show what you do to Black if you get control of the center.

GIUOCO PIANO

WHITE	BLACK		WHITE	BLACK
1 P—K4	P—K4		3 B—B4	B—B4
2 N—KB3	N—QB3		4 P—B3	. . . .

2

White intends to form a broad Pawn center with P—Q4.

Black must fight for the center here by playing 4 . . . N—B3, attacking White's King Pawn. Then, after 5 P—Q4, PxP; 6 PxP, B—N5ch; 7 B—Q2, BxBch; 8 QNxB, P—Q4! Black has successfully achieved a foothold in the center.

Instead, Black loses his way in a clumsy line of play:

4	Q—K2	8 P—QR4	P—QR3
5 P—Q4	B—N3	9 N—R3	B—N5
6 Castles	N—B3	10 N—B2	Castles(K)
7 R—K1	P—Q3	11 N—K3!	....

White's powerful Pawn center stifles Black's pieces and deprives them of adequate scope.

(Note how effectively White's Knight has reached the center by a roundabout route.)

If now 11 . . . B—KR4; 12 N—B5! drives back the Black Queen.

And if 11 . . . BxN; 12 PxB, PxP; 13 N—B5! again drives back the Queen.

So Black's Queen Bishop makes a sorry retreat all the way back.

11	B—B1	13 B—KN5	PxP
12 N—Q5!	Q—Q1	14 PxP	B—N5

3

Black desperately hopes to consolidate his position with . . . BxP.

White's pin on Black's King Knight threatens to rip up Black's King-side with fatal effect. In order to get the most out of the pin, White advances his King Pawn, thus making use of his overwhelming Pawn center:

15 P—K5!	BxN		18 BxN	PxB
16 QxB!	NxQP		19 Q—R6	Resigns
17 Q—KR3	PxP			

Black surrenders because after the coming 20 NxKBPch he will have to give up his Queen to stop checkmate.

White won this game by exploiting Black's failure to enforce a timely . . . P—Q4, which would have given him a fair share of the center.

In the next game, Black again neglects to fight for the center with . . . P—Q4. White soon crushes him in an even more brutal manner.

SICILIAN DEFENSE

WHITE	BLACK		WHITE	BLACK
1 P—K4	P—QB4		6 B—K2	B—N2
2 N—KB3	P—Q3		7 B—K3	Castles
3 P—Q4	PxP		8 P—B4	N—B3
4 NxP	N—KB3		9 N—N3	B—K3
5 N—QB3	P—KN3		10 P—N4!	. . . .

4

White will get an overwhelming position unless Black counters energetically with . . . P—Q4!

10 .... N—Q2??

White can now start a savage Pawn-storming attack which opens up lines of attack against Black's King. After 10 . . . N—Q2?? White is not hampered by any Black counterplay.

11	P—KR4!	P—B4
12	P—R5!	N—B4
13	RPxP	RPxP
14	NPxP	PxP
15	Q—Q2!	PxP

16	Castles (Q)	NxNch
17	BPxN	R—B1
18	QR—N1	B—B4
19	B—B4ch	P—K3
20	Q—R2!	Q—B3

White is ready for the final attack.

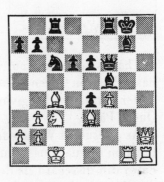

5

White's brilliant sacrifices make the most of his open lines.

21	N—Q5!!	PxN
22	BxQPch	B—K3
23	BxBch	QxB

24	RxBch!	KxR
25	Q—R7ch	K—B3
26	R—R6 mate	

In this game we have seen how White punished Black for neglecting the center.

In the game that follows, White builds up an overwhelming center that is the keystone of a winning attacking formation. Black's opening lapses contribute to the formation of this center.

NIMZOINDIAN DEFENSE

WHITE	BLACK		WHITE	BLACK
1 P—Q4	N—KB3		4 P—K3	P—Q4
2 P—QB4	P—K3		5 P—QR3	BxNch?
3 N—QB3	B—N5		6 PxB	Castles

6

White has the makings of a mighty center formation.

Thanks to Black's faulty exchange on the fifth move, White has a Pawn on Queen Bishop 3. This Pawn strengthens White's center formation by giving additional protection to White's Queen Pawn.

As a result of White's fourth move, his King Pawn had the function of guarding White's Queen Pawn. But now the King Pawn can disregard its defensive job. White therefore forms the plan of advancing P—K4 (move 16!).

In order to play P—K4 White needs several preparatory moves. In the following play, he supports the intended P—K4 with moves 8, 9, 11, 12, and 14.

Once the White Pawn arrives at King 4, White will have a strong Pawn center that will batter down Black's weakened resistance.

7 PxP	PxP		12 P—B3	Q—B2
8 B—Q3	P—QN3		13 BxB	NxB
9 N—K2	B—R3		14 Q—Q3	N—N1
10 Castles	P—B4		15 B—Q2	N—B3
11 N—N3	R—K1		16 P—K4!	. . . .

A very difficult situation for Black. If he captures White's King Pawn with his Queen Pawn, then White recaptures with his King Bishop Pawn. This maintains White's overwhelming center and opens up the King Bishop file for White's attack.

Black therefore stands pat in the center. White continues powerfully with P—K5, *chasing away Black's last protective piece on the King-side.*

16	QR—Q1		18 P—KB4!	N—R4
17 P—K5!	N—Q2		19 N—R5	P—N3

7

The stage is set for a dynamic concluding attack by White.

20 P—B5!!	PxN		23 B—N7ch	RxB
21 B—R6!	K—R1		24 PxRch	K—N1
22 P—B6	R—KN1			

After 24 . . . KxP White has the same winning reply.

25 RxP!!	Q—B3 *		27 Q—B5	N—QB3
26 QR—KB1	Q—R3		28 RxN	Resigns

For if 28 . . . RxR; 29 Q—B8 mate.

A wonderfully instructive game. A comparison of Diagram 6 with Diagram 7 shows clearly how the formation of White's

---

* After 25 . . . KxR; 26 QxP White threatens to obtain a new Queen with discovered—and double!—check. On 26 . . . R—KN1; 27 R—KB1ch wins easily.

overwhelming center left Black with a steadily deteriorating game.

In the next game White wins convincingly when Black runs into trouble by mistakenly giving up a snug defensive position in the center.

QUEEN'S INDIAN DEFENSE

WHITE	BLACK		WHITE	BLACK
1 P—Q4	N—KB3		5 Castles	QN—Q2
2 N—KB3	P—QN3		6 QN—Q2	P—K4
3 P—K3	B—N2		7 P—K4	PxP?
4 B—Q3	P—Q3		8 NxP	P—N3?

White has the makings of a powerful attacking position, thanks to two serious blunders by Black.

Black's seventh move has opened up the game and brought a White Knight to a good post in the center.

Black's eighth move is another lapse. White's Knight at Queen 4, cooperating with his Bishop at Queen 3, is now able to invade Black's territory with menacing effect.*

9 B—N5!   P—QR3   10 B—B6   Q—B1

8

White now follows up with an astonishing advance in the center, made possible by Black's faulty seventh move.

---

* Black should have played 8 . . . P—QR3 in order to prevent the following invasion by White's Bishop.

11 P—K5!!	PxP	13 NxB	B—Q3
12 Q—B3!	BxB	14 N—B4!	....

9

White has prevented 14 . . . Castles, which loses the Black Queen after 15 NxB, PxN; 16 N—K7ch etc.

14	P—K5	16 Q—B3!	Q—N2
15 R—K1	P—R3	17 NxBch	PxN

As a result of the surrender of the center on move 7, White has completely disorganized Black's game. White now wins back his Pawn.

18 RxPch!	K—B1	20 B—B4	QR—QB1
19 R—K7!	K—N2	21 Q—QN3	....

White threatens mate on the move.

21	P—Q4	23 RxPch	K—N1
22 N—K5	QR—K1	24 Q—N3!	....

(See Diagram 10 on page 10.)

White sees that Black cannot guard against the mate by 24 . . . NxN. That would lose Black his Queen, so he tries a last desperate resource, but White winds up brilliantly.

10

Again White menaces mate on the move.

24	P—KN4
25 BxP!	RxN
26 BxN dis ch	KxR

27 Q—N7ch	K—K3
28 BxR	Resigns

White threatens QxR as well as R—K1 with devastating effect. Black has paid a heavy price for giving up the center at move 7.

In each of the games in this chapter we have seen how White has punished Black for giving up control of the center. Throughout the rest of this book you will see repeatedly how important it is to maintain a foothold in the center.

Chapter Two

HOW TO EXPLOIT
YOUR SUPERIOR MOBILITY

YOU WILL FIND, almost without exception, that when you have the better development, your pieces have more mobility than your opponent's forces. Remember that the first move gives you a springboard for getting ahead in development—and for having more mobility than Black has.

Mobility, as you saw in the first chapter, is connected with having a powerful position in the center. The stronger your position in the center, the more mobility your pieces will have. In the following game White emphasizes this point very strongly.

ALEKHINE'S DEFENSE

WHITE	BLACK		WHITE	BLACK
1 P—K4	N—KB3		3 P—Q4	P—Q3
2 P—K5	N—Q4		4 P—QB4	N—N3

Black has developed one piece, White hasn't developed any at all. Yet White has considerable mobility, as his center Pawns dominate the center and many avenues of development are open to his pieces.*

---

* Black's lead in development is academic, as his Knight can accomplish very little from Queen Knight 3.

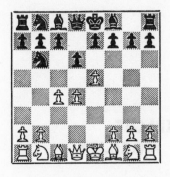

11

Though Black is ahead in development, White has more mobility!

White's immediate aim is to support his powerful Pawn center by advancing his King Bishop Pawn.

5 P—B4	PxP	7 B—K3	B—N2
6 BPxP	P—KN3	8 N—QB3	P—QB4

The advance of Black's Queen Bishop Pawn is logical, as it breaks up the center. (On 9 P—Q5, BxP; 10 BxP Black has a playable though clearly inferior game, as his Knight at Queen Knight 3 is sadly lacking in mobility.)

Instead, Black tries to win a Pawn outright. The attempt is disastrous, because White leaves Black with an unbearably cramped position. White now makes admirably effective use of his superior mobility.

9 P—Q5	Q—B2?	12 NxQPch	K—B1
10 P—Q6!	PxP	13 NxB!	NxN
11 N—N5!	Q—K2	14 BxP!!	Resigns

An extraordinary finish. If 14 . . . QxB; 15 Q—Q8 mate. Thus White wins the Queen by force.

White succeeded admirably in this game because Black started an attack on White's center and failed to follow it up. This gave White time to exploit his superior mobility to the utmost.

12

White is still behind in development and ahead in mobility.

The remaining games in this chapter are more orthodox, for White has superior development, superior mobility, and control of the center in each case.

FRENCH DEFENSE

WHITE	BLACK	WHITE	BLACK
1 P—K4	P—K3	3 N—QB3	PxP
2 P—Q4	P—Q4	4 NxP	....

13

White's dominating position in the center makes it likely that he will have vastly superior mobility in the middle game.

White has a free hand in the center, thanks to Black's colorless third move.

White's Knight is strongly centralized at King 4; his Queen Pawn controls the important center square King 5.

4	N—Q2	7 Castles	NxN
5 N—KB3	KN—B3	8 BxN	N—B3
6 B—Q3	B—K2	9 B—Q3	....

White's game is noticeably freer.

| 9 .... | P—QN3? * | 11 N—B6 | Q—Q3 |
| 10 N—K5! | Castles | 12 Q—B3! | .... |

Very clever. White threatens to win a whole Rook by 13 NxBch.

If 12 . . . B—N2?; 13 NxBch and White wins a piece.

Black must therefore develop his Queen Bishop to Queen 2, where it has no mobility. Thus White's lead in mobility becomes even more pronounced.

12	B—Q2	15 KR—K1	KR—K1
13 NxBch	QxN	16 Q—R3!	....
14 B—KN5	QR—B1		

Now White threatens 17 BxN followed by 18 QxRPch.

14

White's pressure against Black's King-side is irresistible.

White's superior mobility has provided him with a devastat-

---

* Black's position is cramped, but he can at least make a fight of it by playing 9 . . . P—B4.

ing King-side attack. If now 16 . . . P—KR3; 17 **BxP!**, PxB; 18 QxRP and Black is helpless against the coming 19 R—K5 and 20 R—KN5ch.

Or if 16 . . . P—N3; 17 Q—R4, K—N2; 18 R—K4! and White's pin leads to Black's downfall after 19 R—KB4.

With his next move Black admits his despair.

16	Q—Q3	19 R—K3	QxP
17 BxN	PxB	20 P—QB3!	Resigns
18 Q—R6!	P—KB4		

If Black retreats 20 . . . Q—N2 or 20 . . . Q—Q3, he must give up his Queen after 21 R—N3. Otherwise, White forces checkmate with 21 R—N3ch etc.

White had an overwhelming advantage in mobility from the third move on as a result of Black's passive play.

In the following game Black fights hard to maintain his grip on the center. But his development is slow and cramped, and White plays with masterly consistency for domination of the open lines.

PHILIDOR'S DEFENSE

WHITE	BLACK	WHITE	BLACK
1 P—K4	P—K4	5 B—QB4	B—K2
2 N—KB3	P—Q3	6 Castles	P—B3
3 P—Q4	N—KB3	7 P—QR4	....
4 N—B3	QN—Q2		

White has already put his finger on the weakness of Black's position:

The development selected by Black is slow, clumsy, and cramped. White notes especially the lack of mobility of Black's Bishops. His King Bishop is blocked by his Queen's Pawn; his Queen Bishop is blocked by his Queen Knight.

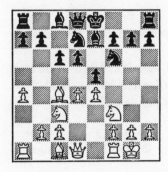

15

White has an advantage in the fact that Black's Bishops have very little scope.

White's policy from now on will be to create more open lines for his own forces and at the same time to restrain Black from freeing himself.

7	Q—B2	12 N—R4!	N—R4
8 Q—K2	P—KR3	13 N—B5	B—B1
9 B—R2	N—B1	14 B—K3	P—KN3
10 Q—B4!	N—K3	15 QR—Q1!!	. . . .
11 PxP	PxP		

White's last move looks like an oversight, but it isn't. He loses no time occupying the open Queen file, even though his Knight is attacked.

This is how White reasons:

As Black has not yet castled, he is unable to bring a Rook to the Queen file to dispute White's occupation of that open line.

Furthermore, because Black's King is still in the center, he cannot hope to win a piece with impunity. Thus if 15 . . . PxN; 16 PxP, N—Q1; 17 N—Q5!, Q—R4; 18 N—N6!!, PxN; 19 RxNch!, KxR; 20 QxKBP and Black's King perishes in the crossfire of the enemy pieces.

This fascinating variation, which deserves the most careful study, is a magnificent example of White's power of superior mobility.

15 ...	B—Q2	18 P—B4!	PxP
16 N—N3	N—B3	19 BxBP	Q—N3ch
17 P—R3	B—N2	20 K—R1	N—R2

White has increased his mobility still more by opening the King Bishop file. Thus he is ready for action on two open files.

16

White can now win by a very brilliant combination.

21 RxB!	KxR	22 B—K3!!	QR—KB1

He might just as well resign. If 22 . . . QxB; 23 RxPch, K—Q1; 24 QxN forces mate.

23 RxPch!!	Resigns

For if 23 . . . RxR; 24 QxNch, K—Q1; 25 BxQch, PxB; 26 QxR and Black is hopelessly behind in material.

White's play was a masterpiece of consistently utilizing superior mobility. From the very start White took merciless advantage of Black's lack of mobility. He never gave Black a chance because he never allowed Black's pieces to cooperate properly.

In the next game White neatly combines superior mobility with control of the center and lasting King-side attack.

WHITE	BLACK	WHITE	BLACK
1 P—Q4	P—Q4	3 N—KB3	N—KB3
2 P—QB4	PxP	4 N—B3	P—K3

White now seizes on the fact that with his second move Black has given up his hold on the center. Black should therefore play . . . P—B4 as soon as possible in order to fight for a foothold in the center. Because he holds back timidly, White gains an overwhelming position in the center by energetic play.

5 B—N5!	B—K2	8 BxP	N—Q2
6 P—K4!	P—KR3?	9 Castles	Castles
7 BxN	BxB	10 P—K5!	B—K2

17

White's formation is aggressive, while the outlook for Black's pieces is very poor.

White has driven a wedge into Black's position by advancing his King Pawn to King 5. One important consequence is that he has prevented Black from bringing his Knight to King Bishop 3. This is the best square for a Knight defending the King-side. It follows that the combination of White's aggressive position in the center, plus the aggressive position of his pieces, foreshadows a powerful attack by White.

Note in the following play how White uses the square King 4 as a steppingstone for transporting his pieces to the King-side. We know from the start that his onslaught will be successful because Black has so little maneuvering space for defensive purposes.

11 Q—K2	R—K1
12 QR—Q1!	P—QB3
13 Q—K4!	Q—B2

14 KR—K1	N—B1
15 Q—N4	P—QN3
16 Q—R5	B—N2

The position begins to look very threatening for Black. White now proceeds to bring more pieces to the King-side. Because of the cramped position of his forces, Black cannot defend with equal vigor.

18

White again gets more pieces into the attack by using the square King 4.

17 R—K4!	B—N5
18 R—N4	BxN
19 PxB	K—R1

20 N—N5!	R—K2
21 N—K4!	R—Q1
22 R—Q3!	P—QB4

At last Black plays the move that he should have played early in the opening. But White is now ready for the final attack, having maneuvered his Knight into position for a deadly stroke. He has also moved his Queen Rook into position for the final attack.

23 N—B6! . . . .

With the brutal threat 24 QxRPch!!, PxQ; 25 R—N8 mate. White's superior mobility has become overwhelming.

Of course, if Black tries 23 . . . PxN then 24 QxRPch and 25 Q—N7 mate.

23	N—N3	24 R—R3	Resigns

19

White has left Black no move to hold the position.

White's overwhelming plus in mobility has left Black without any satisfactory defense.

Thus if 24 . . . PxN; 25 QxPch, K—N1; 26 Q—R8 mate.

Or 24 . . . PxP; 25 Q—N5!!, QxB; 26 RxPch!, PxR; 27 QxP mate.

White never gave Black a chance after Black's all too passive handling of the opening.

In the following game White again triumphs after dominating the center and preventing Black from getting his pieces into action. White's Pawn-storming attack follows with crushing—and logical—effect.

SICILIAN DEFENSE

WHITE	BLACK	WHITE	BLACK
1 P—K4	P—QB4	3 P—Q4	PxP
2 N—KB3	P—Q3	4 NxP	. . . .

White has a well-centralized Knight established at Queen 4. Black cannot imitate this maneuver. Note also that White controls the important center square Queen 5 with his King Pawn.

On these two grounds it seems likely that White will dominate the center and will therefore enjoy superior mobility.

20

There are already strong indications that White may achieve an over-whelming plus in mobility.

4	N—KB3	7 B—K3	B—K2
5 N—QB3	N—B3	8 Castles	Castles
6 B—K2	P—K3		

How has the situation developed as regards mobility? Both White Bishops have free diagonals; both Black Bishops are hemmed in by Pawns. The outlook for Black's game is very unpromising.

In such positions White always has a practical problem: *how can his superior mobility be increased still further?* White solves this problem by a general advance of his King-side Pawns, which will achieve the following:

1. He will congest Black's position more than ever.

2. He will drive away Black's King Knight—his best defensive piece—from King Bishop 3.

3. He will subject Black's position, already cramped unbearably, to a devastating Pawn-storming attack.

9 P—B4	Q—B2	12 P—B5	Q—Q1
10 P—KN4!	P—QR3	13 P—KR4	NxN
11 P—N5	N—K1	14 QxN	....

White's plan has made considerable progress. As a result of Black's unpromising opening line of play, White has deprived Black of any constructive plan.*

21

The formidable centralization of White's Queen provokes Black to lose his foothold in the center.

14 ....   P—K4?

Very shortsighted. He drives away the Queen, but at the cost of permanently losing Pawn control of his Queen 4 square.

This vital center square now becomes a "hole," completely at the mercy of the White pieces.

15 Q—Q2	N—B2		17 R—B2	B—Q1
16 B—N6!	Q—Q2		18 QR—KB1	....

White menaces a decisive breach with 19 P—B6, P—N3; 20 P—R5. Black stops this, but White penetrates in a different way.

18	P—B3		20 P—N6!	P—R3
19 B—B4ch	K—R1		21 B—B7	Q—B3

White can now win by 22 B—K3 and 23 BxP! He plans a much more striking finish.

---

* The continuation . . . B—Q2 and . . . B—QB3 is about the best Black has.

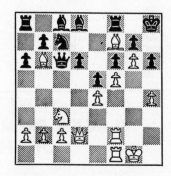

22

There is no defense against White's coming attack.

| 22 BxN | BxB | 23 R—N2! | P—Q4 |

Desperation.

24 QxRPch!!   Resigns

For if 24 . . . PxQ; 25 P—N7ch, K—R2 and now White captures the Rook, promoting to a Knight (!) and giving checkmate after 25 . . . K—R1; 26 R—N8ch!

The games in this chapter teach a lesson of the greatest practical importance—that when White gets the initiative through superior mobility, he has a lasting advantage that he can increase systematically until he achieves victory.

The first step is to pinpoint Black's faulty strategy. Once you see how he has committed himself to a cramped position, you can find ways to increase your command of the board. You must not swerve from your determination to keep him in a vise; one thoughtless move will often allow the enemy to escape. All five games in this chapter show how you maintain and increase the pressure until Black's position collapses.

Chapter Three

HOW TO EXPLOIT BLACK'S PREMATURE OPENING UP OF THE POSITION

THE BANE of many chess books is that they ignore the human factor. You may have read the last paragraphs of the previous chapter with some skepticism. Suppose Black is not satisfied to be trussed up; suppose he fights back? How does White proceed in such cases?

We can approach the problem of cramped positions systematically by dividing such positions into three parts. Those positions in which Black defends passively without any attempt to fight back have been treated in the previous chapter. Positions in which Black tries to open up the position are the subject of the present chapter. Positions in which Black resorts to counterattack will be the subject matter of Chapter Four.

We start with a game in which Black is so anxious to avoid a cramped position that he opens up the game before castling. This transfers the struggle from a predominantly *strategical* one to a predominantly *tactical* one. The switch, as we shall see, favors White.

SICILIAN DEFENSE

WHITE	BLACK	WHITE	BLACK
1 P—K4	P—QB4	4 NxP	N—B3
2 N—KB3	N—QB3	5 N—QB3	P—Q3
3 P—Q4	PxP	6 B—K2	P—K4

This reminds us of Black's fourteenth move in the previous game (after Diagram 21). Black surrenders control of the important square Queen 4. This gives White a powerful hold on the center and foreshadows a serious lack of mobility on Black's part.

23

White intends to train his guns on the weakness created by Black's last move.

7 N—B3	P—KR3	9 Castles	B—K2
8 B—K3	B—K3	10 Q—Q2	P—Q4?

In his anxiety to get a free hand in the center, Black advances forthrightly to get rid of White's control of the Queen 5 square.

Strategically the advance is irreproachable. It has, however, the drawback of provoking a lasting attack by White.

11 PxP	NxP	12 B—QN5!	. . . .

By pinning Black's Queen Knight White threatens NxP. This forces one concession after another by Black.

12	P—B3	15 Q—Q3	R—Q1
13 QR—Q1	NxB	16 Q—N6ch	K—B1
14 QxN	Q—N3	17 RxRch	BxR

If 17 . . . NxR??; 18 Q—K8 mate.
If 17 . . . QxR; 18 BxN, PxB; 19 NxP wins a Pawn.

How to Exploit Black's Premature Opening Up • 25

24

White is operating with brilliant tactical threats.

18 NxP!   B—QB2

White's threats cannot be met satisfactorily: if 18 . . . NxN??; 19 Q—K8 mate. If 18 . . . PxN; 19 QxB and White has a winning game.

19 N—Q5!   Resigns

A magnificent winning move. If 19 . . . QxB; 20 NxB attacking Black's Queen and also threatening 21 Q—K8 mate.
If 19 . . . B/K3xN; 20 N—Q7ch winning Black's Queen.
Thus White faultlessly exploited Black's premature opening up of the position. In the following game Black is strangely inconsistent. First he drifts listlessly into a critically cramped position; then, with equally poor judgment, he strikes out recklessly to achieve freedom. White hits back hard.

KING'S INDIAN DEFENSE

WHITE	BLACK	WHITE	BLACK
1 P—Q4	N—KB3	4 P—K4	P—Q3
2 P—QB4	P—KN3	5 P—KN3	Castles
3 N—QB3	B—N2	6 B—N2	QN—Q2

25

White's pieces are likely to have more mobility than Black's forces.

7 N—B3	P—K4	10 B—K3	N—KN1
8 Castles	P—KR3	11 Q—B2	N—N3
9 P—KR3	K—R2	12 P—N3	P—KB4?

Dissatisfied with the slight scope of his forces, Black opens up the position violently. *But White, having much greater mobility*, reacts with brutal effectiveness.

What makes White's reaction all the more powerful is that Black has loosened up the Pawn position in the vicinity of his King. The result is that it is relatively easy for White to penetrate the Black King's defenses.

| 13 QPxP | BPxP | 14 NxP | N—Q2? |

Black takes advantage of the fact that White's King Pawn is pinned on the long diagonal. But this is trifling compared to White's smashing attack against Black's weakened Kingside.

| 15 N/K4—N5ch! PxN | | 16 NxPch | Resigns |

If 16 . . . K—R3 White wins the Black Queen with 17 N—B7 dbl ch or 17 N—K6 dis ch.

If instead 16 . . . K—R1; 17 QxP, QN—B3; 18 PxN, NxP; 19 N—B7ch, RxN; 20 QxR and White is two Pawns and the Exchange ahead. In the face of this crushing material advantage, Black resigns.

26

White scores a decisive win of material no matter how Black replies.

In this game White profited by Black's cramped game in the opening. Later on, when Black tried to struggle out of his straitjacket, White opened effective lines for his action-greedy pieces.

In the next game Black has a satisfactory opening position, but by thoughtlessly opening up the game he exposes himself to a decisive attack. Again White is alive to the possibilities, and quickly works up a withering attack.

NIMZOINDIAN DEFENSE

WHITE	BLACK	WHITE	BLACK
1 P—Q4	N—KB3	3 N—QB3	B—N5
2 P—QB4	P—K3	4 P—K3	. . . .

27

In this seemingly conservative variation White's Bishops have enormous potential power.

4	Castles	7 N—K2	P—K4
5 P—QR3	BxNch	8 N—N3	P—Q3
6 PxB	R—K1	9 B—K2	QN—Q2

There is a clash of plans here. As in Diagram 6, White wants to open up the position so that his Bishops will have powerful play. Black, on the other hand, should strive to keep the position closed.

| 10 Castles | P—B4 | 12 BPxP! | N—N3 |
| 11 P—B3 | BPxP? * | 13 B—N2 | PxP? |

28

White's Queen Bishop has come to life!

White has been on the alert to increase the scope of his Bishops. He is well aware that Black has gone completely astray with his eleventh and thirteenth moves.

The position is opened up for White's pieces, and this is particularly true of White's Queen Bishop. As you will see, White knows just how to derive the maximum benefit from this.

| 14 P—K4! | B—K3 | 16 QxP | Q—B2 |
| 15 R—B1 | R—K2 | 17 P—B5! | . . . . |

As a result of White's masterly fourteenth move he has

---

* This sadly inconsistent move opens up a future for White's Queen Bishop.

created a magnificent diagonal for his Queen Bishop and powerfully centralized his Queen at Queen 4.

Thus White is supreme in the center and in the general mobility of his forces. All this may be traced back to Black's mistake in prematurely opening up the position on move 11.

With his last move White increases his mobility and prepares to switch a Rook to the King-side. This will lead to a surprisingly quick decision.

| 17 .... | PxP | 19 B—B1! | Q—N1 |
| 18 RxP | Q—B5 | 20 R—KN5! | QN—Q2 |

White was threatening QxN/B6.

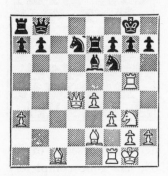

29

White is ready for a bombshell finish.

| 21 RxPch!! | KxR | 22 N—R5ch | K—N3 |

Or 22 . . . K—R1; 23 NxN, Q—K4; 24 B—N2!, QxQch; 25 BxQ, NxN; 26 BxNch winning a Rook.

23 Q—K3!　Resigns

White has foreseen that Black will be helpless against the double threat of 24 Q—R6 mate or 24 Q—N5 mate. He has made Black pay a high price for prematurely opening up the position.

The next game shows a still further refinement of this type of mistake. Black prematurely opens up the position *for his opponent* without even seeking any real or imaginary compensation. White's resulting attack, as we might expect, is devastating.

FRENCH DEFENSE

WHITE	BLACK	WHITE	BLACK
1 P—K4	P—K3	5 QN—K2	P—QB4
2 P—Q4	P—Q4	6 P—QB3	N—QB3
3 N—QB3	N—KB3	7 P—KB4	P—B3
4 P—K5	KN—Q2	8 N—B3	. . . .

The very nature of this opening gives White a much freer position. His pieces have more scope, and Black's Queen Bishop is hemmed in for good.

However, White does not have a completely free hand; Black is keeping the White center under pressure by attacking it with his King Bishop Pawn and Queen Bishop Pawn.

Since this is all the pressure that Black has, he ought to increase it by playing 8 . . . Q—N3. By keeping White's center under observation, Black would distract White's attention from his attacking intentions.

30

*White is now greatly relieved as Black deprives himself of his **only** counterplay.*

8	QBPxP?	12 B—K3	N—N3
9 BPxP	B—N5ch	13 B—Q3	N—B5
10 N—B3	PxP?	14 BxN	PxB
11 BPxP	Castles	15 Castles	N—K2

White has the better development and superior mobility. Black is limited to a passive role.

| 16 Q—K2 | BxN | 18 N—N5! | B—Q2 |
| 17 PxB | Q—B2 | 19 Q—R5 | P—KR3 |

White has suddenly built up a powerful attack. Black's last move seems to give him a respite, but White has a surprising reply.

20 R—B7!!   ....

Apparently a losing move in view of the possible reply 20 . . . B—K1.

But White has a remarkable resource in answer to 20 . . . B—K1, namely 21 RxPch!!, KxR; 22 NxPch, K—N1; 23 Q—N4ch followed by 24 NxQ with a crushing material advantage for White.

| 20 .... | Q—Q1 | 21 QR—KB1 | N—B4 |

31

White has a brilliant concluding combination.

Black has managed to block the open King Bishop file, but White is not impressed. He has concentrated his forces so powerfully on the King-side that he can afford spectacular sacrifices.

22 R(B1)xN!	PxR	27 Q—R6ch	K—B2
23 RxPch!	KxR	28 BxQ	QRxB
24 N—K6ch!	BxN	29 Q—B6ch	K—N1
25 BxPch	K—R2	30 QxBch	K—N2
26 B—N5 dis ch	K—N2	31 Q—K7ch	Resigns

White will advance his passed Pawns in the center to achieve a quick victory by queening a Pawn.

Thus White has made magnificent use of the open King Bishop file presented him by Black's premature opening up of the position.

In each of the games in this chapter Black has opened up the position prematurely. Through this opening up he has made it possible for White to develop an overwhelming attack.

This type of mistake is frequently made in over-the-board play. Consequently the methods adopted in these games by White are of the greatest practical value. By refuting these premature actions, White successfully defends his initiative.

Chapter Four

HOW TO EXPLOIT
BLACK'S PREMATURE COUNTERATTACK

IN THE PREVIOUS CHAPTER we saw how White won consistently by taking advantage of Black's prematurely opening up the position. White, generally being the player with the better development, is generally in position to benefit by the opening of lines.

Premature counterattack presents a much sharper problem. Here Black not only opens up lines—he actually *attacks*. If White reacts carelessly to a premature opening up of the position, he loses his initiative. If he reacts carelessly to a premature counterattack, *he may well lose the game*.

The following games show in an impressive way how White *can react effectively* to such premature counterattacks.

EVANS GAMBIT DECLINED

WHITE	BLACK	WHITE	BLACK
1 P—K4	P—K4	5 P—QR4	P—QR3
2 N—KB3	N—QB3	6 P—R5	B—R2
3 B—B4	B—B4	7 P—N5	PxP
4 P—QN4	B—N3	8 BxNP	N—B3

Black has an excellent development and he is now ready to castle into safety. "This won't do!" says White, and he plays to confuse Black with complicated possibilities.

9 B—R3!? ....

This crafty move provokes Black to embark on a counter-attack which looks very attractive because it involves a powerful threat.

By playing . . . NxKP, Black threatens a decisive gain of material with . . . NxBP. Yet White is untroubled. He has looked further ahead and has prepared suitable counter-measures.

(Black should play 9 . . . P—Q3, shunning the complications.)

9	NxKP?	11 NxP!	N—Q5
10 Q—K2!	NxBP	12 NxQP dis ch!!	

White's last move seems incomprehensible at first sight. We might even take it for despair, in view of Black's fourfold threat of . . . NxQ or . . . NxR or . . . NxB or . . . NxPch. (Note that 12 QxN??—instead of the move actually played—would not do at all because of 12 . . . NxPch winning White's Queen.)

32

White gives up his Queen . . . and wins outright!

12	NxQ	13 N—B6 mate!

White had to be exceptionally resourceful to refute Black's plausible and promising counterattack.

Such premature counterattacks are favorites with daring and aggressive players who are aware that bluff is a potent weapon in chess. When the player of the White pieces is equally daring and has superior development in his favor, the counterattack is likely to grind to an abrupt halt. Here is another case in point:

QUEEN'S GAMBIT

WHITE	BLACK	WHITE	BLACK
1 P—Q4	P—Q4	4 P—K3	PxP
2 P—QB4	PxP	5 PxP	B—N5?
3 N—KB3	P—QB4	6 BxP	. . . .

Threatening 7 BxPch, KxB; 8 N—K5ch coming out a Pawn ahead with a winning position.

From this variation you can see that White realizes the early development of Black's Bishop is ill-judged. But Black is determined to counterattack; White must hit hard to keep his initiative.

6	P—K3	8 N—K5	QxP!?
7 Q—R4ch!	N—QB3	9 NxN	Q—K5ch

The only move, as he obviously cannot play 9 . . . PxN?

10 B—K3	PxN

Forced, for if 10 . . . QxN??; White pins and wins the Queen with 11 B—QN5.

11 N—B3!	QxP	12 B—Q5!!	. . . .

A complete sermon in one move. White forcefully separates Black's Queen from Black's King. The effect of White's brilliant Bishop move is that Black's premature counterattack disappears in graceful fireworks.

33

White's brilliant 12 B—Q5!! seizes the initiative.

12	KPxB	15 Q—N7ch	K—K3
13 QxBPch	K—Q1	16 Q—B6ch	B—Q3
14 QxRch	K—Q2	17 B—B4!!	Resigns

A spectacular finish. After 17 . . . QxRch; 18 K—Q2, QxR; 19 QxBch White mates in two more moves.

White has pitilessly punished Black's premature counterattack which took his Queen hopelessly far afield.

In the following game when Black commits the same mistake, White's punishment is even more forceful.

VIENNA GAME

WHITE	BLACK	WHITE	BLACK
1 P—K4	P—K4	3 B—B4	B—B4
2 N—QB3	N—QB3	4 Q—N4?!	....

This early development of the Queen is wrong on principle. Black's best reply is doubtless 4 . . . K—B1, protecting his King Knight Pawn and threatening to win a piece with . . . P—Q4. Black would thereby lose the castling privilege but would gain time by his attacking threat.

Defending and attacking at the same time. Black is so taken with the false economy of this move that he fails to provide for White's ingenious reply.

5 N—Q5!!	QxPch	6 K—Q1	K—B1

White's powerful Knight move has left Black nothing better against the double threat of 7 NxPch or 7 QxNP. So Black has had to move his King after all. White has even more formidable threats in store for him.

7 N—R3	Q—Q5	8 P—Q3	B—N3

White was threatening to trap Black's Queen by 9 P—B3!! He has used Black's premature counterattack to box in Black's Queen, which now offers no help to the Black King.

But this is not all: White can now operate on the open King Bishop file, thanks to Black's premature attack with the Queen. This enables White to win quickly by a spectacular, incisive attack.

9 R—B1!   N—B3

White's threat was 10 NxB, RPxN; 11 RxPch and Black can resign.

34

White is ready to embark on a brilliant sacrificial attack.

10 RxN!   P—Q3

White's sacrifice of the Exchange is based on the idea that
if 10 . . . PxR; 11 B—KR6ch, K—K1; 12 Q—N7 the King
Rook cannot be saved. Black tries a different way, but White's
refutation is sensational:

11 QxPch!!!	KxQ	13 R—N6ch!!	RPxR
12 B—KR6ch	K—N1	14 N—B6 mate!	

Rarely do we see such a convincing refutation of a premature counterattack as White has provided here. The next
example is much more difficult for White because the counterattack seems to be based on a fairly reasonable idea. Nevertheless, White sees that Black's counterplay is basically unsound. White follows up that observation with forceful, daring
play.

QUEEN'S GAMBIT

WHITE	BLACK	WHITE	BLACK
1 P—Q4	P—Q4	4 P—K3	P—B4
2 P—QB4	PxP	5 BxP	PxP
3 N—KB3	N—KB3	6 PxP	Q—B2?

This premature development of the Queen is definitely out
of place, as White has many ways to defend his attacked
Bishop.

White deliberately selects a method that will provoke an
unsound counterattack by Black.

7 Q—N3!   B—K3??

The very move that White wanted to provoke! Black is
under the impression that White cannot capture this Bishop
because of the reply . . . QxBch, winning at least a piece.

35

White is about to give Black an unpleasant surprise!

8 BxB!!	QxBch
9 K—K2	QxR
10 BxPch	**K—Q1**

11 QxP	Q—B8
12 QxR!	QxPch
13 QN—Q2	N—K5

Now the full depth of White's plan is revealed.

Black's last move is a shamefaced admission that his counterattack has misfired. In reply to 13 . . . QxR there follows 14 QxNch, K—Q2; 15 N—K5 mate.

The move actually chosen is not much of a help, either.

| 14 QxN/K4 | QxR |
| 15 Q—Q5ch | K—B2 |

| 16 Q—B5ch | K—Q1 |
| 17 B—K6 | Resigns |

For if 17 . . . N—Q2; 18 Q—B6, N—N3; 19 N—K5 followed by N—B7 mate.

From these games we can see that premature counterattack by Black generally takes the form of an early Queen development. Once this happens, White can generally entice the Black Queen far afield. If this requires substantial offers of material, don't shrink from making them—*provided you can see genuine compensation to reward your sacrifices.*

Chapter Five

HOW TO EXPLOIT BLACK'S WEAKENING PAWN MOVES

THIS IS a very profitable subject. Familiarity with it will yield you many victories. This is why:

When your opponent weakens his position with ill-judged Pawn moves, he obviously does not know such moves are weakening. If he had that knowledge, he would of course avoid the Pawn moves.

Hence it follows that once Black has weakened his position, he has left himself wide open to powerful moves by which you can take advantage of his weakness. The following games tell you what you need to know in order to take advantage of weakening Pawn moves.

FRENCH DEFENSE

WHITE	BLACK	WHITE	BLACK
1 P—K4	P—K3	5 N—K4	P—KB4?
2 P—Q4	P—Q4	6 N—N5!	B—K2
3 N—QB3	N—KB3	7 N/N5—B3	P—B3
4 PxP	NxP	8 N—K5	....

Black's weakening Pawn advance at move 5 has ruined his position. This move has left a backward Pawn on the King file: the Black King Pawn cannot be defended by Pawns.

White exploits this by posting his Queen or a Rook—or both—on the King file.

Equally disastrous for Black is the fact that Black's fifth move has left his King 4 square a "hole"—a square that Black can no longer protect by Pawn moves.

This makes it possible for White to occupy the "hole" with a Knight. *Posting a Knight on a vital center square* in this fashion is one of the strongest possible moves on the chessboard.

In this first part of the game, White has succeeded in bringing a Knight to the important square. The second part of the game will show you what happens as the result of White's aggressive placement of the Knight.

36

White controls the center as a result of Black's faulty fifth move.

8	Castles		11 Castles	R—K1
9 N/N1—B3	P—QN3		12 P—B4	N—B3
10 B—Q3	B—N2		13 B—B4	QN—Q2

White's ninth and thirteenth moves have both strengthened his powerful hold on the center. He continues that policy with his next move—a very important one, as we shall see.

14 Q—K2   P—B4

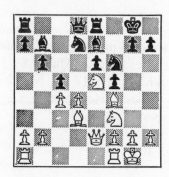

37

White now plays one of the most surprising moves ever made on the chessboard.

15 N—B7!!! ....

White has not left Black much choice in replying to this amazing move. If he removes his Queen from attack by playing 15 . . . Q—B1, White replies 16 QxP, confiscating the King Pawn. (This is the Pawn weakened by Black's feeble fifth move.)

After this capture, White is threatening a murderous double check. If Black tries 16 . . . K—B1; 17 N/B7—N5 is decisive.

15 ....   **KxN**   16 QxPch!!! ....

38

White has captured the weak King Pawn in spectacular fashion.

Black's weakening move now leads to his downfall. If 16

. . . KxQ; 17 N—N5 mate! This possibility vividly illustrates White's powerful control of the center.

Refusing the Queen by 16 . . . K—B1 is futile, for then White plays 17 N—N5 with crushing effect.

Black tries another way, but White forces mate in two moves.

16 . . . .   K—N3   17 P—KN4!   B—K5
                    18 N—R4 mate

The way in which White exploited the weakening of Black's Pawn position was very instructive. In the next game White does an equally good job in taking advantage of a Pawn weakness created by Black.

FRENCH DEFENSE

WHITE	BLACK	WHITE	BLACK
1 P—K4	P—K3	5 N—B3	B—Q3
2 P—Q4	P—Q4	6 B—Q3	Castles
3 N—QB3	N—KB3	7 Castles	N—B3
4 PxP	PxP	8 B—KN5	. . . .

By pinning Black's King Knight, White threatens NxP.

39

White has given Black a troublesome problem: how is he to defend his Queen Pawn?

| 8 .... | N—K2?? * | 10 N—KR4! | K—N2 |
| 9 BxN | PxB | 11 Q—R5! | .... |

Black's faulty eighth move has breached his King-side Pawn position. White naturally trains his guns on the gap in Black's castled position.

It is clear that White is taking admirable advantage of the opportunities offered. He has brought a Knight and the Queen into aggressive play. From now on, White keeps bringing more and more pieces to the King-side. In this way White builds up an imposing concentration of force against the Black King.

11	R—R1	14 QR—KB1	Q—B2
12 P—B4	P—B3	15 N—K2!	B—Q2
13 R—B3	N—N3	16 N—N3	QR—KN1

40

White's concentration of force on the King-side is so overwhelming that he can afford to sacrifice his Queen.

To appreciate White's brilliant combination, bear in mind that it is based on Black's *weakening of his Pawn position.*

17 Q—R6ch!!!	KxQ	20 P—N4ch!	KxP
18 N/R4—B5ch	BxN	21 R—N3ch	K—R4
19 NxBch	K—R4	22 B—K2 mate	

---

* Black's best way to meet the threat is 8 . . . B—KN5, counterattacking against White's Queen Pawn.

How to Exploit Black's Weakening Pawn Moves • 45

Striking as this combination is, what really interests us is that White did a masterly job in taking advantage of the gap in Black's King-side.

In the next game, White shows equal skill in exploiting the same kind of weakness in Black's King-side.

QUEEN'S GAMBIT DECLINED

WHITE	BLACK	WHITE	BLACK
1 P—Q4	P—Q4	7 R—B1	P—B3
2 P—QB4	P—K3	8 B—Q3	PxP
3 N—QB3	N—KB3	9 BxBP	N—Q4
4 B—N5	B—K2	10 BxB	QxB
5 P—K3	QN—Q2	11 Castles	NxN
6 N—B3	Castles	12 RxN	P—K4

Starting out with a cramped position—the kind we have studied in Chapter Two—Black has worked hard to free himself.

41

White must fight hard to maintain the initiative.

White must be extremely alert now to maintain some initiative.

13 NxP	NxN	15 P—B4	Q—K2? *
14 PxN	QxP	16 P—B5	P—QN4

---

* Black should have played 15 . . . Q—B3.

White's further advance of his King Bishop Pawn will break up Black's King-side Pawn position. Thus White will stamp Black's sixteenth move as a serious mistake.

| 17 B—N3 | P—N5 | 18 P—B6! | . . . . |

42

White breaks up Black's King-side.

White has put his finger on the weakness created by Black's faulty fifteenth move. White's advance of the King Bishop Pawn opens up a dangerous gap on the King-side. From now on, White concentrates his forces more and more powerfully against Black's King.

Note that this process of gathering concentration is typical. First, you pinpoint the weakness. Second, you switch your forces to bear on the weakened point. Third, you deploy your superior forces to crush Black's weakened resistance.

18	PxP	22 Q—Q2	K—R1
19 QRxP	QxPch	23 BxP	QR—B1
20 K—R1	B—N2	24 R/B6—B2	QR—Q1
21 QRxP	Q—K5	25 Q—N5!	R—Q3

White has skilfully brought his pieces to bear on the exposed Black King. His last move threatened 26 Q—B6 mate.

43

White's magnificently posted pieces are poised for the final attack.

26 B—Q5!!   Resigns

A brilliant final move. White offers his Bishop three ways and attacks three pieces. Black cannot guard his attacked Rook and attacked Queen at the same time and he must therefore resign.

An interesting possibility is 26 . . . RxR so that if 27 RxR???, Q—K8ch leading to mate. However, on 26 . . . RxR White plays 27 Q—N8 mate.

In the next game Black weakens his white squares. White's exploitation of this weakness is a masterpiece of positional maneuvering.

RUY LOPEZ

WHITE	BLACK		WHITE	BLACK
1 P—K4	P—K4		7 B—N3	P—Q3
2 N—KB3	N—QB3		8 P—B3	Castles
3 B—N5	P—QR3		9 P—Q3	B—K3
4 B—R4	N—B3		10 QN—Q2	N—KR4
5 Castles	B—K2		11 P—Q4!	BxB
6 R—K1	P—QN4		12 PxB	. . . .

Black's game is somewhat cramped but it is free from weaknesses. As in the previous game, White must be alert for opportunities to preserve some initiative.

12	....	N—B5	15	P—Q5!	N—Q1
13	N—B1	Q—B1?	16	BxN!	PxB
14	N—N3	P—N3	17	N—K2	P—N4

One glance at Diagram 55 shows that White's sixteenth move was a masterpiece.

44

White has his strategic goal clearly laid out for him: Black is now very weak on the white squares.

Black made a mistake in allowing his Knight to be exchanged. White showed masterly judgment in making this exchange, which compels 17 . . . P—N4 on the following move.

What White has achieved is that a number of white squares in Black's position are no longer protected by Black Pawns. White's success is particularly notable because of his control and coming occupation of the King Bishop 5 square.

White's interpolation of 15 P—Q5! was another admirable stroke. He drove back Black's Knight at a time when the Knight had to retreat to the Queen 1 square. At this post the Knight is badly out of play, which will handicap Black in the coming phase.

As we know from previous games, White's next step is *to concentrate his forces for attack*. He devotes his next three moves to posting his Knights aggressively and unassailably.

| 18 N/B3—Q4 | R—K1 | 19 N—B5 | B—B1 |
| 20 N/K2—Q4 | .... | | |

45

Neither of White's powerfully posted Knights can be driven away.

Now that White has established his Knights firmly, his next step is to open the King Rook file. This will enormously increase the attacking potential of his position.

| 20 .... | P—KB3 | 22 RPxP | P—B4 |
| 21 P—N3! | PxP | 23 N—B3 | N—B2 |

White has purposely retreated his Knight because he intends to use it for his King-side attack. The next stage in White's build-up of pressure is to attack on the newly opened King Rook file.

24 N—R2!	R—R2	28 NxQP!	R—Q1
25 Q—R5	B—N2	29 NxN	PxN
26 N—N4	Q—Q2	30 N—B5	B—B3
27 K—N2	N—K4	31 R—R1	R—KB1

(See Diagram 46.)

32 Q—N4!   ....

46

White is now ready for the final attack.

White proceeds with the final regrouping of his forces. The immediate threat is 33 RxQRP!, RxR; 34 N—R6ch winning Black's Queen!

32	....	K—R1		35 QR—R1	R/B1—B2
33	R—R6	P—R4		36 Q—B5	Q—KB1
34	N—K3!	Q—K1		37 N—N4	B—Q1

White now announced mate in three moves: 38 RxPch, K—N1 and now 39 Q—N6ch and 40 R—R8 mate.

The way that White broke through on the open King Rook file from the position of Diagram 46 is most instructive. Looking back over the earlier part of the game, you can appreciate the importance of his opening of the King Rook file by 21 P—N3! You can also see how useful it was for White to force the weakening of the white squares by 16 BxN!

This game is particularly valuable because White has done such a convincing job in exploiting the weaknesses in Black's position. Unlike most of the games in this book, the game had very little in the way of brilliancy. Yet White was in full command of the situation; he pushed his advantage to the utmost.

So far in this chapter we have been studying White's procedure against weaknesses on Black's King-side or in the neighborhood of his King. But weaknesses on the Queen-side,

How to Exploit Black's Weakening Pawn Moves • 51

far away from the King, can also be disastrous. Here is an impressive example:

QUEEN'S GAMBIT DECLINED

WHITE	BLACK		WHITE	BLACK
1 P—Q4	P—Q4		5 B—N5	QN—Q2
2 P—QB4	P—K3		6 P—K3	Castles
3 N—QB3	N—KB3		7 R—B1	P—QN3
4 N—B3	B—K2			

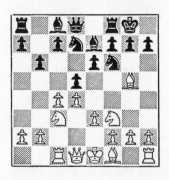

47

White has a marked positional advantage because Black has created a "hole" at his Queen Bishop 3 square, which can no longer be protected by a Pawn.

White now sets himself to take advantage of the weakness at Black's Queen Bishop 3 square. Here is White's plan of campaign:

First he plays PxP in order to clear the Queen Bishop file for pressure by his Queen Rook against the weakened point. (Later on you will be able to appreciate the power of this pressure.)

White's next step will be to exchange the white-squared Bishops. In this way he will eliminate the Black Queen Bishop which would have been able to protect the weakened point.

8 PxP!	PxP		11 QxB	P—B3
9 Q—R4!	B—N2		12 Castles	N—K5
10 B—QR6!	BxB		13 BxB	QxB

White's plans have proceeded according to schedule. Black's weakened Queen Bishop 3 has been replaced by a weak Queen Bishop Pawn, and White now turns his attention to this Pawn.

48

White is now ready to pounce on the weak Pawn.

14 Q—N7!   KR—B1   15 NxP!   Q—Q3

After 15 . . . PxN; 16 RxRch White is the Exchange and a Pawn ahead, with an easy win.

16 RxP!!   Resigns

White's last move is a brilliant stroke which wins more material than Black can afford to part with. For if 16 . . . QxN?; 17 RxRch wins the Queen.

And if 16 . . . RxR; 17 QxQRch, N—B1; 18 QxR!!, QxQ; 19 N—K7ch followed by 20 NxQ leaves White a Rook ahead.

Finally, if 16 . . . QxR?; 17 N—K7ch wins the Queen.

In this game White carried out his strategical ideas with attacking moves. In the final game of the chapter he operates with strictly strategic methods. While less spectacular, this policy is equally effective.

How to Exploit Black's Weakening Pawn Moves   •   53

QUEEN'S GAMBIT DECLINED

WHITE	BLACK		WHITE	BLACK
1 P—Q4	P—Q4		4 N—B3	B—K2
2 P—QB4	P—K3		5 B—N5	Castles
3 N—QB3	N—KB3		6 Q—B2	QN—Q2

Even at this early stage White has an inkling of what course the game may take. Black's Queen Bishop is badly hemmed in. White must keep a sharp eye on that Bishop in the hope of keeping the Bishop tied up permanently.

7 R—Q1	P—B3		12 BxP	P—QN4
8 P—K3	P—KR3		13 B—R2	Q—N3
9 B—R4	P—R3		14 Castles	B—N2
10 P—QR3	R—K1		15 N—K5!	QR—Q1?
11 B—N3	PxP		16 P—N4!!	. . . .

White takes advantage of Black's faulty fifteenth move.*

49

White now has a winning positional advantage.

With his last move White has established a lasting bind on the position. By preventing . . . P—B4 for good, he has stamped Black's Queen Bishop Pawn as *a backward Pawn on an open file.* In all the intricate maneuvering that follows,

---

* Black should have freed his Queen Bishop with . . . P—B4.

White keeps his eye on this Pawn and finally piles up enough force to capture it.

But White enjoys still another advantage after 16 P—N4!! He keeps Black's Queen Bishop hemmed in for good. This means that to all intents and purposes White is playing with a piece ahead.

16	P—QR4		19 N—B5	N—B1
17 N—Q3!	PxP		20 B—N1	B—B1
18 PxP	R—R1		21 P—R3	N—Q4

Now that White has pinpointed the weakness, he goes on to the next phase: piling up on the weakness. First comes a very fine Knight maneuver aimed at transferring his Knight from Queen Bishop 3 to Queen Rook 5. At this latter post the White's Knight will bear down on the weak Queen Bishop Pawn.

22 N—R2!	R—R2		25 N/B1—N3	N—B3
23 P—K4	N—B3		26 N—R5	N—R4
24 N—B1	N/B3—Q2		27 B—KR2	P—N3

White has posted his Knights to the best advantage. His next four moves lead to the capture of the weak Pawn.

28 Q—B3!	B—B3		30 B—K4!	R—B2
29 P—K5!	B—K2		31 Q—B3!	

50

White must now win the weak Queen Bishop Pawn.

31	B—Q2	34 P—Q5!	N—N1
32 NxB	NxN	35 PxP!	NxN
33 NxP	B—B1	36 BxN	RxP *

White has achieved his aim. He now goes on to make use of his superior mobility.

37 B—Q5!	N—N2	43 R—R1	Q—B1
38 BxR	NxB	44 R—R8	Q—B8ch
39 R—Q6!	BxR	45 K—R2	P—B3
40 PxB	R—Q2	46 QxP	N—N2
41 R—Q1	K—R2	47 Q—B8	P—N4
42 B—K5	Q—R3	48 BxN!	Resigns

After 48 . . . RxB White mates by 49 Q—B5ch, R—N3; 50 R—R7ch, K—R1; 51 Q—B8ch! etc.

The games in this chapter give us a very clear and thorough method for White's procedure against weaknesses. The earlier White recognizes these weaknesses, the better for him. Even at a very early stage of the game, they give him a target to aim at; they provide a complete plan of the game. Once the target is created, White need not drift or guess; by concentrating on the target, he is playing the strongest and most logical moves.

---

* If Black captures the Bishop, the reply 37 PxPch is deadly.

Chapter Six

HOW TO EXPLOIT
BLACK'S ERRORS OF JUDGMENT

ERRORS OF JUDGMENT, like weakening moves, enable you to train your forces on a target. Errors of judgment on Black's part provide you with a ready-made plan of attack.

However, you have to be alert to note these errors of judgment. If the lapse is ignored, Black may very possibly escape without serious damage. In each of the following games White is well aware of the lapse as soon as it happens, and vigorously turns it to his advantage.

In the first game, Black makes a plausible move that ruins his chances of achieving a normal development. White's method of exploiting this error of judgment is simple but highly effective.

The simplifying variation White adopts in this game is rather deceptive. Black is set for an easy game, but White knows how to create unexpected difficulties.

FOUR KNIGHTS' GAME

WHITE	BLACK		WHITE	BLACK
1 P—K4	P—K4		4 B—N5	B—N5
2 N—KB3	N—QB3		5 Castles	Castles
3 N—B3	N—B3		6 BxN	. . . .

51

White will get his big opportunity as Black proceeds to make an error of judgment.

6 ....   NPxB?

By capturing with the Queen Pawn, Black opens up a line of development for his Queen Bishop.

The text, on the contrary, blocks the Bishop's development.

Here White sees his chance—*to make use of the superiority in development that he is bound to obtain because Black's Queen Bishop is immobilized.*

| 7 NxP | R—K1 | 9 PxB | NxP |
| 8 P—Q4 | BxN | 10 R—K1! | .... |

Very powerful. White's Rook move creates serious difficulties for Black. If 10 . . . N—B3; 11 B—N5 gives White a lasting and annoying pin. If 10 . . . NxQBP; 11 Q—B3 and White attacks the Knight and also threatens QxKBPch.

10 ....   N—Q3

Now Black's Queen Pawn·cannot move, and it is not clear how his Bishop is to be developed. Credit this to White's pressing Rook move. White has made important progress by ruining Black's prospects of development.

In the following stage White builds up strong pressure on the King-side, which lacks proper protection.

11 Q—N4!   Q—B3

If 11 . . . P—B3; 12 B—R6, P—N3; 13 NxNP! and
White wins.

| 12 B—R3 | R—Q1 | 13 R—K3! | . . . . |

While Black works hard to unscramble his pieces, White
increases his pressure on the King-side. Note the helplessness
of Black's Bishop.

| 13 . . . . | N—B4 | 15 Q—R5 | P—N3 |
| 14 R—B3 | P—Q4 | 16 N—N4! | Q—R1 |

A queer-looking move, but White has the whip-hand in any
event because of his powerful accumulation of forces on the
King-side.

52

*White's lead in development is now
decisive.*

| 17 Q—N5 | B—K3 | 18 RxN! | Resigns |

For if 18 . . . BxR; 19 N—R6ch, K—N2; 20 NxBch,
K—N1; 21 B—K7 threatening to win the Queen with 22
B—B6 or to win a Rook with 22 BxR.

White timed his play perfectly to take advantage of Black's
error of judgment on move 6. By continuing to pile on pres-

sure relentlessly on the King-side, White emphasized the backwardness of Black's development.

In the next game White deals with a somewhat different kind of error on Black's part. Starting out with a reasonably satisfactory development, Black undermines the position of his most effective piece.

White must ask himself such questions as: Where is Black's error of judgment? How can I take advantage of that error?

VIENNA GAME

WHITE	BLACK		WHITE	BLACK
1 P—K4	P—K4		3 P—B4	P—Q4
2 N—QB3	N—KB3		4 BPxP	NxP

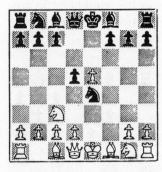

53

White must contend with a powerfully centralized Black Knight.

At a very early stage in the game, White has a serious problem: what is he to do about the effectively posted Black Knight in the center? Exchanging Knights is not aggressive enough, so White spars for time.

5 N—B3	B—QN5		8 Q—K3	N—QB3
6 Q—K2	BxN		9 B—Q3	P—B4
7 NPxB	Castles		10 Castles	P—B5

A critical move which unhinges the support of Black's well-posted Knight.

11 Q—K2   N—N4?

This is the mistake White has been waiting for.* The centralized Knight leaves his powerful post. At the same time Black's far advanced King Bishop Pawn becomes an exposed weakness.

12 B—R3!   NxNch   13 QxN!   R—B2

White is playing with superb tactical skill. In reply to 13 . . . NxP he plays 14 Q—R5, attacking the Knight, threatening BxPch with a mating menace, and keeping Black's Rook under attack.

14 QR—K1   . . . .

White's alert play has brought all his pieces into powerful play. His Bishops are magnificently trained for attack. Thus, if now 14 . . . B—K3 (to hold back the threatening King Pawn) White continues 15 Q—R5, P—KN3; 16 BxP!, PxB; 17 QxPch winning the Bishop with two Pawns to the good.

14 . . . .   P—KN4

To guard the advanced Bishop Pawn and to defend the King Rook Pawn against Q—R5.

But White has all the play and now forces the game in a few moves.

15 P—K6   R—N2   16 Q—R5!   . . . .

Now White has the brutal threat 17 P—K7!, NxP; 18 BxN, RxB; 19 QxNPch, K—B1; 20 RxPch, K—K1; 21 Q—N8ch, K—Q2; 22 QxQPch, K—K1; 23 R—B8ch!

---

* 11 . . . B—B4 supports the well posted Knight.

16	N—K2	17 B—QB5!	N—B3

He cannot allow White to play B—Q4.

54

White crowns his masterly attack by breaking up Black's position.

18 P—K7!	NxP	19 BxN	Resigns

If 19 . . . RxB; 20 QxNPch and White wins as in the note to White's sixteenth move.

This game is extremely impressive because of the way that White worked up a devastating attack after Black's error of judgment. White's removal of Black's Knight from the center opened up the lines that White needed for the effective cooperation of his forces.

In the next game, a wrong opening choice by Black leaves him exposed to White's tactical threats. White maneuvers very cleverly to take advantage of the opportunities offered.

FRENCH DEFENSE

WHITE	BLACK	WHITE	BLACK
1 P—K4	P—K3	5 PxP	QxP
2 P—Q4	P—Q4	6 BxN	BxNch
3 N—QB3	N—KB3	7 PxB	PxB
4 B—KN5	B—N5	8 N—B3	....

55

White wants to drive off Black's centralized Queen.

In order to drive away Black's Queen from an effective centralized post, White plans to play P—N3 followed by B—N2 with threats against the Black Queen.

8	P—N3	9 P—N3	B—N2
	10 B—N2	Q—KR4? *	

White threatened 11 N—R4 with decisive effect. Black has avoided this threat, but he has put his Queen out of play. White will make good use of the Queen's inactive role.

11 Castles	N—Q2	14 N—R4!	BxB
12 Q—K2	QR—B1	15 NxB	PxP
13 Q—K3!	P—QB4	16 PxP	....

White's Pawn sacrifice is neatly calculated. After 16 . . . RxP; 17 Q—R3!!, P—R4; 18 QR—B1, RxR; 19 RxR White has reduced his opponent to helplessness. (White would then threaten R—B8 mate, and Black would be unable to castle out of danger.)

In offering this variation, White relies on the inactive role of Black's Queen.

---

* Black gets an equal game with . . . Q—K5ch, which practically forces White to agree to the exchange of Queens by 11 Q—K2 etc.

16	Castles		19 P—KB3!	Q—N4
17 Q—K4	R—B2		20 R—B2	R—Q1
18 N—B4	Q—N5		21 P—KR4!	Q—R3

If 18 . . . QxNPch?; 19 R—N2 pins and wins the Queen.

White now begins a very ingenious maneuver to harry the Black Queen and at the same time to exploit the lack of harmony among Black's forces.

| 22 P—N4! | QxP | | 23 R—R2 | Q—N4 |

After 23 . . . Q—N6ch; 24 K—R1 White can confidently look forward to trapping the Black Queen.

56

White can capture the King Rook Pawn, but he has an even stronger move.

| 24 NxP!! | PxN | | 25 QxKPch | .... |

Now you can see how White's unexpected combination takes advantage of the lack of communication among Black's forces. If 25 .... K—B1; 26 Q—Q6ch wins a Rook. The same is true of 25 . . . K—N2; 26 Q—K7ch.

Black tries a different defense, but White's superior mobility still tells in his favor.

25	K—R1		28 QxRch	N—B1
26 Q—K7	Q—N1		29 QxNch	Q—N1
27 RxPch!	QxR		30 QxPch	Resigns

White has succeeded admirably in carrying out his original aim of exploiting the lack of cooperation between Black's Queen and his other pieces. Black's loss of material makes further resistance hopeless.

In the following game it is up to White to punish his opponent for a slight transposition of moves toward the beginning of the middle game. It is very instructive to see how White carries out this idea.

NIMZOINDIAN DEFENSE

WHITE	BLACK	WHITE	BLACK
1 P—Q4	N—KB3	4 P—K3	Castles
2 P—QB4	P—K3	5 P—QR3	BxNch
3 N—QB3	B—N5	6 PxB	P—Q3

Here White faces the same kind of problem as in the play following Diagram 27. He wants open lines for his pieces—particularly the Bishops—while Black's interests are best served by a closed position.

57

White needs open lines for his coming attack.

7 B—Q3	P—B4	10 Castles	P—QN3
8 N—K2	N—B3	11 P—B4	B—R3? *
9 P—K4	N—K1!	12 P—B5!	P—K4

---

* By playing 11 . . . P—B4! Black would have avoided the terrific attack that follows.

White has just the kind of position he was aiming for, thanks to Black's carelessness at move 11. White can now force a breach in Black's King-side position and just keep on piling up pressure against Black's game. In this way he takes advantage of the fact that Black's pieces are poorly placed for defensive purposes.

58

White can force a weakness in Black's King-side by a very surprising move.

13 P—B6!!

This amazing move breaks up Black's King-side no matter how he plays.

After 13 . . . NPxP; 14 B—R6 White has achieved his objective. Black's King-side formation is then similar to the one in Diagram 40. The Black King is exposed to attack, and White simply continues to bring additional pressure to bear. (The actual continuation of the game proceeds along similar lines.)

If Black tries 13 . . . NxBP White can still inflict the unwieldy doubled Pawn on him by playing 14 B—N5. White would then have lasting pressure by means of the pin supported by his Rook on the open King Bishop file.

13	K—R1	14 P—Q5	N—R4
	15 N—N3!	....	

White's Knight now comes into play very strongly. He is indifferent to the loss of a Pawn by 15 . . . BxP; 16 BxB, NxB for after 17 PxPch, NxP; 18 B—R6 his attack rolls on undiminished.

| 15 . . . . | PxP | 17 Q—R5 | BxN |
| 16 N—B5 | B—B1 | 18 PxB | R—KN1 |

To force a clearly winning position White only needs to bring his King Rook into the attack.

This he now proceeds to do, applying the formula which has been used so often by White in these games. First he determines where the weakness lies; then he concentrates his forces on the weak spot; finally, he attacks in overwhelmingly superior strength.

In this case the weakness is Black's exposed King-side, *created by White's brilliant thirteenth move.*

19 R—B3!   . . . .

Threatening mate in four moves beginning with 20 QxRPch!!

| 19 . . . . | R—N2 | 21 R—R3 | N—KN2 |
| 20 B—R6 | R—KN1 | 22 Q—R4! | Resigns |

Black is helpless against the coming 23 B—N5, P—R4; 24 QxPch!!, NxQ; 25 RxNch, K—N2; 26 B—R6ch and mate next move.

The power of White's concluding attack has amply proved the correctness of White's judgment in making the surprising Pawn advance on move 13.

In this last game, as in all the games in this chapter, we have seen how White takes advantage of Black's error of judgment. The important requirement, as far as White is concerned, is alertness. If White is watchful enough to see how Black's plans are spoiled by a hasty move, then that observation is half the battle.

Nor can White afford to be dogmatic. He applies whatever attacking methods are needed to refute Black's play, and he does not mind changing his plans as the occasion requires.

Thus, in this game, White wanted originally to get good attacking diagonals for both Bishops. Yet after his twelfth move White had to reconcile himself to the fact that his white-squared Bishop was destined to play a minor role. There were two reasons why White accepted this philosophically.

In the first place, the Pawn moves that shut in *this* Bishop (9 P—K4 and 13 P—B6!!), opened the diagonal for White's black-squared Bishop. Secondly, Black had so many inactive pieces that the blocking of the King Bishop was of minor importance.

This kind of elasticity is an important quality in a chess-player. We're often told that a plan is important; unfortunately, we hear less often that a plan needs modifying as the original conditions are modified. In all the games in this chapter, White is very sensitive to *the changes in Black's policy that are the results of errors of judgment*. The result, as you have seen, is effective attack and quick victory.

Chapter Seven

HOW TO EXPLOIT IRREGULAR DEFENSES

WHEN WE HAVE the White pieces, we generally start with
1 P—K4 as a matter of course. Why this is advantageous
has already been pointed out in the first chapter.

Now, suppose Black avoids the expected reply (1 . . .
P—K4) and plays some unorthodox move, such as 1 . . .
P—KN3 or 1 . . . P—QN3. This leads to a mysterious kind
of opening play, quite different from the familiar consequences of 1 P—K4, P—K4.

Once Black plays these strange defenses, the pieces do
not come into contact with each other so readily. There is a
great deal of portentous maneuvering. Such an opening, to
a player who has no clear idea of his opening goals, can be
a very trying affair.

But above all, there is a psychological factor that enters
into this kind of play: the element of dread. White may take
for granted that this strange defense must be good; it must,
he reasons, have all sorts of virtues that are unknown to him.
These unorthodox defenses are even described sometimes as
"secret weapons"!

It is no exaggeration to say that for many players, being
confronted with these unusual defenses is enough to spoil
the game for them. They are baffled by the problem of
building up the position logically: they don't know what to
expect, and in any case they blindly fear the worst.

Before we go on to study some of these defenses and to see how easily and effectively they can be refuted, we must dwell for a moment on the kind of attitude that is characteristic of the resourceful chessplayer. He never assumes that a surprising move is *necessarily good*. Like any other move, it may be good or bad. Like any other move, it must be weighed on its objective merits.

Hence the resourceful chessplayer is not taken aback by an unsual defense. He tries to see what it can achieve; he tries to plan his own procedures against it. Here knowledge and experience are important. The greater understanding a player has of chess, the less likely he is to be awed by an unusual defense.

The fact is that these unusual defenses *are* inferior lines of play, highly disadvantageous for Black. It is precisely for this reason that they are unusual. The standard openings are the ones that have been approved by experience and theoretical analysis.

If these unusual defenses are inferior, why are they played? There are three main reasons. One is sheer ignorance on the part of the player of the Black pieces. He may not know that these defenses are bad. This implies that he is a poor player. Certainly this possibility should encourage us, rather than fill us with foreboding.

Secondly, it may be that the player of the Black pieces is afraid of the more orthodox lines of play. For some reason he does not feel at home in them, or lacks the confidence that he can do well with them. So he resorts to bizarre lines in order to take his opponent "out of the books." This motivation, too, is one that need not make us uneasy. For again we see that Black is in difficulties before he makes his first move. We can await the future with confidence.

The third possibility is that Black is a good player and well knows that his unusual defense is inferior. Why then does he play it? Just to confuse the issue—to evoke a mood of discomfort in his opponent.

Let this then be our point of departure. If we have a clear idea of the defense and its weaknesses, we have nothing to fear.

Controlling the center

Experience has shown, as we know, that the two strongest opening moves are the double advance of the King Pawn (1 P—K4) or the double advance of the Queen Pawn (1 P—Q4). And, as far as most players are concerned, it is best for Black to answer 1 P—K4 with 1 . . . P—K4 and to answer 1 P—Q4 with 1 . . . P—Q4.

The basic reasons for these moves were indicated in the first chapter. Here we go much more deeply into the analysis of the importance of the center.

If you place a Queen on one of the four center squares on the chessboard (either King 4 square or either Queen 4 square), you will find that on the open board the Queen has a choice of 27 moves. Place her on other squares, and the number of possible moves decreases. The farther you move her from the center, the fewer moves are available to her.

Repeat the experiment with a Knight. At a center square he has 8 possible moves. In a *corner* square he has only 2 possible moves.

How about a Bishop? On a center square he has 13 possible moves; on a *corner* square he has only 7.

The moral is clear. The center is the area where the pieces have their greatest striking force, their greatest mobility. As they move away from the center, their power decreases. Poised at the center or near it, they stand ready to move quickly to any sector of the board, and are able to reach either flank quickly.

How is this affected by playing out the center Pawns

early? We have seen that it is desirable to occupy (or to control) the center squares: King 4, King 5, Queen 4, Queen 5—reckoning from either side. If White plays 1 P—K4, he controls—commands—the vital center square Queen 5. That is to say: if Black plays his Queen or any other piece to that square, White's King Pawn can capture it. Therefore, by playing 1 P—K4 White prevents Black pieces from occupying an important center square. From what we have read earlier in this chapter, this means that the mobility of Black's pieces is reduced.

When White's King Pawn reaches the King 4 square, it also controls the King Bishop 5 square. This is just off the center and is therefore a fairly important square. By controlling it with his King Pawn, White deprives the Black pieces of access to that square.

Now that White has played 1 P—K4 and controls the Queen 5 and King Bishop 5 squares, White has a formidable strategical threat: he threatens 2 P—Q4, obtaining a broad Pawn center. If his opponent permits this, White will in addition control the vital center square King 5, and he will also control the valuable Queen Bishop 5 square.

In that case White's pieces will have free access to the center, whereas his opponent's forces will be barred from it. *Consequently White's pieces will have more mobility than those of his opponent.*

Now we can take stock of the problem that confronts Black after 1 P—K4. What move must he play in order to get his fair share of center control and to assure his pieces of equal access to the center? The answer is clear: he must follow White's example and advance his King Pawn two squares, by playing 1 . . . P—K4. In this way he maintains equality.

Suppose, however, that Black neglects to play 1 . . . P—K4 or some other move that takes up the struggle for control of the center. This brings us to the unusual defenses—the ones that give Black a bad game because they bypass the problem of controlling the center. And they give him a bad game for a second reason which derives from the first—*the player who lacks control of the center cannot develop his pieces effectively*.

Given these two discouraging conditions, the outlook for Black's game is necessarily bad. Consequently, the player of the White pieces need never be discouraged when he is confronted with one of these inferior defenses; in fact, he should be elated. He has splendid winning prospects, right from the start.

Defenses with . . . P—KN3

In this type of defense, Black fianchettoes his King Bishop; that is, he plays . . . P—KN3 followed by . . . B—N2. The result is that he cedes all control of the center to White; in addition, Black is burdened with a slow, clumsy development. He is on the defensive from the very beginning, and he is often in considerable danger.

And White? He monopolizes the center with his King Pawn and Queen Pawn. He has a variety of good development systems for his forces. The initiative is his birthright, and the whole orientation of his game is aggressive.

KING'S FIANCHETTO DEFENSE

WHITE	BLACK
1 P—K4	P—Q3

It is clear that this move is too passive. Black fails to control the vital Queen 5 square. He allows White's Queen Pawn to advance unimpeded.

2 P—Q4   . . . .

White accepts the invitation. Now he has the broad Pawn center, making it impossible for Black's pieces to find a firm foothold in the center.

Note also that White has opened the diagonals of both his Bishops.

$$2 \ldots \qquad N—Q2$$

This is development of a sort, but it is cramping and picayune. (The Knight would hit harder at the center if developed at Queen Bishop 3. Note also that 2 . . . N—Q2 blocks the development of Black's Queen Bishop.)

$$3 \text{ B—QB4} \qquad \ldots$$

White has reason to be satisfied with his powerful position. He has now developed his King Bishop on an aggressive diagonal.

Note that this Bishop aims directly at Black's King Bishop Pawn. This Pawn, or the square on which it stands, is often the target for White's attack. This is especially true when White has an aggressive position while Black's game is crowded and undeveloped.

$$3 \ldots \qquad P—KN3$$

Black continues with bizarre moves, instead of playing 3 . . . P—K4 in order to establish his King Pawn belatedly in the center.

$$4 \text{ N—KB3} \qquad \ldots$$

Developing another piece. White's development is far more powerful than Black suspects. In fact, even at this early stage White menaces a devastating combination, thanks to Black's inept failure to contest the center and to develop his pieces effectively.

Now Black has fianchettoed his Bishop as planned.

But even at this early stage White has a winning continuation.

59

Black's game is already compromised.

5 BxPch!   ....

At once White makes use of his vastly superior position. Of course, if Black sees what is coming, he can decline the Bishop by 5 . . . K—B1. But in that case he would be a Pawn down and, having moved his King, he could never castle. His position would be chaotic, his King in danger, his development in arrears. In short, White would have a won game with his material advantage and attacking possibilities.

5 ....   KxB   6 N—N5ch   ....

This powerful check wins by force.

On 6 . . . K—B1 White has 7 N—K6ch winning the Black Queen with a Knight forking check. (This underlines the inadvisability of 2 . . . N—Q2, blocking the Black Queen Bishop.)

How to Exploit Irregular Defenses • 75

And on 6 . . . K—K1 there follows 7 N—K6 winning the Black Queen because she has no flight square.

6 ....   K—B3   7 Q—B3 mate

Seven moves and it is all over! Clear proof that Black's defensive system was very bad.

White had an easy time of it. All he had to do was to make good use of the superior mobility which was presented to him by Black's inferior defense.

Defenses with ... P—QN3

Here Black fianchettoes his Queen Bishop at once, without putting up any preliminary fight for control of the center. Once more White has a free hand, achieving a powerful development and a sweeping initiative.

QUEEN'S FIANCHETTO DEFENSE

WHITE	BLACK	WHITE	BLACK
1 P—K4	P—QN3	2 P—Q4	....

Taking advantage of Black's neglect of the center, White has established a broad Pawn center. This will soon result in phenomenal activity for the White pieces.

2 ....   B—N2

Developing the Bishop and attacking White's King Pawn. But such sporadic and uncoordinated attacks have no real power.

3 B—Q3   ....

White develops his Bishop effectively and at the same time guards his King Pawn.

3 ....   P—KB4?

This astonishingly thoughtless move has a kind of mad consistency behind it. Black sets an obvious trap: if 4 PxP, BxP and Black wins a Rook.

But Black completely forgets that by moving his King Bishop Pawn while his game is still undeveloped, he is exposing himself to disaster.

4 PxP!! ....

White "falls" into the trap. With his Queen and his King Bishop poised for attack, he has a crushing refutation.

4 .... BxP

According to plan. But his pleasure is short lived.

5 Q—R5ch ....

The point that Black missed. As a result of his premature advance of the King Bishop Pawn, he has exposed his King to a relentless attack.

5 .... P—N3 6 PxP ....

Now White threatens 7 P—N7 mate or 7 PxP mate. That such a violent threat is available at such an early stage indicates how badly Black has played the opening. It is also a tribute to the power of White's central Pawn advances.

6 .... N—KB3

At last some development—but it is much too late.

On some such move as 6 . . . P—Q3 (to give the Black King a flight square), there would follow 7 P—N7 dis ch followed by 8 PxR/Q, leaving White with an overwhelming advantage in material.

How to Exploit Irregular Defenses • 77

60

White wins by a beautiful Queen sacrifice.

White's onslaught is so fierce that he can even afford to sacrifice his Queen:

7 PxP dis ch!   NxQ   8 B—N6 mate

A sensational finish like this one certainly poses a moral. Black ignored the problem of controlling the center; he failed to develop his King-side pieces; he indulged in a premature attack before his development was properly under way; he exposed his King to a fatal attack.

White, on the other hand, built up a broad Pawn center that gave his pieces scope for attacking play; his sacrifices on moves 4 and 7 were only Greek gifts.

The future will always belong to the player who has the stronger center position and the better development—though perhaps not in such a spectacular form as here. Therein lies the great flaw of these unusual—and inferior—defenses: they give White a commanding lead at the very start.

Inferior Defenses after 1 ... P—K4

Even if Black answers 1 P—K4 with 1 . . . P—K4, he can still go wrong very quickly by playing some unusual move frowned upon by theory. One such move, which turns up rather frequently, is an early . . . P—KB3.

When the average player, with the White pieces, encounters this move he is puzzled. It never appears in the books, or in the games of good players. It looks solid enough, for its obvious purpose is to guard Black's Pawn on King 4.

And yet the early . . . P—KB3 is a very bad move, invariably compromising Black's game, and giving White an opportunity for decisive action.

Here is a convincing case in point:

DAMIANO GAMBIT

WHITE	BLACK		WHITE	BLACK
1 P—K4	P—K4		2 N—KB3	P—KB3?

The right move is 2 . . . N—QB3. In that way Black develops a piece, guards his King Pawn, and brings the Queen Knight to a post from which it strikes at the center.

3 NxP!   ....

This dynamic capture demonstrates that Black's last move was wrong. If now 3 . . . PxN; 4 Q—R5ch (again this ominous move) and Black must choose between 4 . . . P—KN3; 5 QxKPch which cost him a Rook or 4 . . . K—K2; 5 QxKPch, K—B2; 6 B—B4ch which exposes him to a mating attack.

The prime defect of . . . P—KB3? is, then, that it weakens the position of the Black King. A lesser but still substantial defect is that Black's King Knight is deprived of its best square for development.

3 ....   Q—K2

Black tries a different way. It avoids immediate disaster, but it has the drawback of developing the Queen prematurely and exposing her to attack by White's pieces.

| 4 N—KB3 | P—Q4 | 6 PxP | QxPch |
| 5 P—Q3 | PxP | | |

Thus Black has regained the Pawn, but meanwhile White develops his pieces rapidly. Sooner or later he will gain time by menacing the Black Queen.

| | 7 B—K2 | B—KB4 |

Threatening . . . QxP.

| 8 P—B3 | B—Q3 | 9 B—K3 | N—K2 |

Black is striving to develop his pieces with commendable rapidity, and is just on the point of castling his King into safety. But White's alert reply spoils everything.

| 10 QN—Q2 | . . . . |

Gaining time by attacking Black's Queen.

The choice of a reply is difficult, for after 10 . . . Q—K3 White can play 11 B—QB4 (hitting at Black's Queen again), Q—Q2; 12 N—Q4 and Black is in great trouble, as he cannot castle. Thus the consequences of . . . P—KB3? continue to plague Black.

| 10 . . . . | Q—KN5 |

This looks harmless, yet White is now in a position to win the wandering Black Queen.

61

Black's Queen is trapped!

11 N—KN1!!   ....

Incredible as it may seem, this demure retreat wins Black's Queen or else establishes an equivalent material advantage.

Thus, if 11 ... Q—N3; 12 B—R5 traps the Black Queen. (The early ... P—KB3? still takes its toll.)

And if 11 ... QxP; 12 B—B3 wins on the spot, as Black is left without a good move.

11 ....   Q—KR5   12 P—KN3!   Resigns

White has trapped the Black Queen on the open board; a drastic demonstration of the drawbacks to an early ... P—KB3?

This chapter has shown that the unusual defenses are unusual because they give Black a bad game. They neglect the problem of center control; they neglect the problem of mobility; they neglect the problem of commanding adequate terrain.

Because of these defects in Black's game, White can get a winning position by appropriate techniques: by monopolizing control of the center; by developing his pieces quickly and effectively; by working up attacks that are bound to win by a quick decision against Black's ineffectual development.

Chapter Eight

HOW TO SEIZE THE INITIATIVE

IF YOU ACCEPT the view that White has some initiative by reason of his first move, you will doubtless agree that in actual practice White often loses that initiative with great rapidity.

And, furthermore, if you realize just what is happening, you will be in a position to snatch up White's lost initiative and become the aggressor.

Now, assuming that White does not lose material and does not create weaknesses, just what should Black look for in order to seize the initiative?

There are several ways White can go wrong. He may, for example, play an opening so poor that his theoretical advantage disappears at once. This gives Black his chance.

Or White may play an excellent opening and then ruin his development by a series of foolish, time-wasting Queen moves. Here again Black must be alert to the possibilities.

If Black discovers that White is wasting valuable time chasing a relatively unimportant Pawn, he can use the opportunity to get far ahead in development.

Sometimes White may avoid the sin of greed only to succumb to another fault—bad judgment. Sheer thoughtlessness, inattention, negligence, or happy-go-lucky innocence of a positional trap may ruin White's development. In every case Black should be alert to seize the initiative.

So you see there are many ways for White to go wrong,

and it pays Black to keep a sharp lookout for such cases of poor judgment. Now let's see some examples of the kinds of mistakes White may make.

Lost initiative from a poor opening

In this game Black gives us a classic example of slashing attacking play. His play is magnificent, and yet—it all stems from White's faulty opening. Black immediately pounces on the opportunities offered by White's faulty play.

IRREGULAR OPENING

WHITE	BLACK		WHITE	BLACK
1 P—QN4	P—K3		2 B—N2	N—KB3

Even at this early stage we can see the faulty character of White's first move. Black is attacking, White is defending! Black's development will proceed rapidly, while White's will be laborious.

| 3 P—QR3 | P—B4 | | 4 P—N5 | P—Q4 |

Black's Pawns already have a substantial foothold on the center, while White has no Pawns in the center at all. His attempt to improve the situation leads to disaster.

5 P—Q4?   ....

Plausible but weak, as Black promptly proves.

62

Black now seizes the initiative.

5 ....   Q—R4ch!

This forceful move starts a chain reaction. It forces White to play N—QB3 in order to protect his unfortunate Queen Knight Pawn. Then, to protect this Knight, White is forced to develop his Queen in a risky manner. These factors give Black his chance for a brilliant attack.

| 6 N—QB3 | N—K5 | 8 QxP | B—B4! |
| 7 Q—Q3 | PxP | 9 QxNP | BxPch |

Black's brisk attacking play has shunted White's Queen far from the scene of action and has deprived White's King of the castling privilege. Even at this early stage White's position is shattered.

10 K—Q1   ....

63

How does Black guard his menaced Rook?

10 ....   P—Q5!!

Black ignores the attack on his Rook because he has decided on an all-out attack on the White King. Note, by the way, that 11 NxN? allows 11 . . . Q—K8 mate!

| 11 QxRch | K—K2! | 12 QxB | PxN |

In the event of 13 BxP Black intends 13 . . . NxBch; 14 K—Q2, N—K5 dbl ch; 15 K—Q3, Q—Q7ch; 16 KxN, Q—K6 mate.

13 B—B1   N—Q2!!

64

Black offers another Rook!

Black has calculated the play very closely. Thus if now 14 Q—B4, R—Q1; 15 Q—N4ch, QN—B4 dis ch!; 16 B—Q2, RxBch; 17 K—B1, R—Q8ch!!; 18 KxR, Q—Q1ch followed by mate.

What now follows is a foregone conclusion, despite White's enormous material advantage. With four powerful attacking pieces at his disposal, Black engineers a sparkling mating attack.

14 QxR	QxNP	16 K—B1	B—K6ch!!
15 B—B4	Q—Q4ch	17 BxB	N—B7!!

White resigns, for after 18 BxN Black replies 18 . . . Q—Q7ch forcing mate in two more moves.

Black has forcefully punished White for losing the initiative by choosing an inferior opening line.

Lost initiative from too many Queen moves

In the next game White starts out with an excellent opening; but then, animated by some perverse suicidal impulse, he lets his Queen drift out of play. Black develops rapidly and forcefully, sacrifices both Rooks, and wins handsomely.

NIMZOINDIAN DEFENSE

WHITE	BLACK		WHITE	BLACK
1 P—Q4	N—KB3		5 PxP	N—R3
2 P—QB4	P—K3		6 P—QR3	BxNch
3 N—QB3	B—N5		7 QxB	NxP
4 Q—B2	P—B4		8 B—N5	P—QR4

65

A typical situation in the Nimzoindian Defense.

This position is typical of the opening because Black has developed rapidly but has had to give up one of his Bishops in the process.

White should now play 9 P—B3, P—R5; 10 P—K4, P—Q3 leading to a position with chances for both sides. Instead, his weak play enables Black to seize the initiative.

9 Q—K5?	P—Q3		11 Q—B4?	P—K4
10 BxN	PxB		12 Q—R6	Q—N3!

Black has gained two moves for developing his Bishop and

has also brought his Queen into active play. White belatedly returns to rational moves, but as Black demonstrates, it is already too late for that.

| 13 R—N1 | B—B4!! | | 15 QxRch | Q—K2 |
| 14 QxBP | BxR | | 16 QxR | .... |

66

Black has a mating attack.

This is the position Black has played for: White's Queen is far afield, and his other pieces are still on their home squares.

16 ....   N—K5!

Threatens mate in two.

17 P—K3   QxNP

Threatening mate on the move.

18 QxRP   QxBPch

White resigns, for if 19 K—Q1, QxBch; 20 Q—K1, Q—Q6ch and mate next move. Black has played with superb energy to exploit White's nerveless loss of the initiative.

Lost initiative from greedy play

In the next game, also, White plays the opening not too badly but Black maneuvers ingeniously to obtain the advantage when White becomes greedy.

FRENCH DEFENSE

WHITE	BLACK		WHITE	BLACK
1 P—K4	P—K3		5 B—Q3	B—Q3
2 P—Q4	P—Q4		6 Castles	Castles
3 PxP	PxP		7 N—B3	N—B3
4 N—KB3	N—KB3		8 B—KN5	....

White has already forfeited part of his initiative by playing 3 PxP and thereby opening the diagonal of Black's imprisoned Queen Bishop. Nevertheless, Black is still under some pressure, mainly because his King Knight is pinned and his Queen Pawn is under attack.

67

How is Black to defend his Queen Pawn?

Black's daring conclusion is that he need not defend his Queen Pawn altogether!* Therefore he plays:

---

*In a similar game (pages 44-45) Black played the timid 8 . . . N—K2??; 9 BxN, PxB; 10 N—KR4! and was roundly trounced a few moves later.

8 ....   B—KN5!

The first point of Black's play is that if 9 NxP, BxPch;
10 KxB, QxN and he has recovered the Pawn with a good
game.

9 BxN   QxB!   10 NxP   Q—R3!

Now Black threatens 11 . . . BxN and 12 . . . QxP mate.
Nor can White defend with 11 P—KN3?, for then 11 . . .
Q—R4! wins.

True, White can play 11 Q—B1, but after 11 . . . QxQ;
12 QRxQ, BxN; 13 PxB, NxP Black has regained his Pawn
and has a very promising endgame. White therefore selects
what *seems* to be the least evil:

11 P—KR3   ....

68

Black has seized the initiative.

11 ....   NxP!

Black offers a piece that cannot be accepted, for if 12
PxB???, NxNch; 13 QxN, Q—R7 mate.

12 B—K2   NxNch   13 BxN   BxP!

Black, who gave up a Pawn a few moves ago, is now actually a Pawn ahead. White cannot play 14 PxB because of 14 . . . QxP; 15 R—K1, B—R7ch; 16 K—R1, B—N6 dis ch; 17 K—N1, Q—R7ch and mate next move.

14 R—K1	B—K3	16 Q—K2	BxN
15 P—KN3	QR—Q1	17 BxB	BxP!

A neat thrust. If 18 PxB, RxB with a second Pawn to the good.

18 B—K4	R—Q7	19 QxR	B—R7ch!

White resigns, for if 20 K—N2, QxQ; 21 KxB, QxKBPch with a tremendous advantage in material for Black.

Lost initiative from blocked development

It was fascinating to see how cleverly Black snatched the initiative and the attack in this bright little game. In the next game all is tranquil throughout, but the game is if anything even more instructive.

FOUR KNIGHTS' GAME

WHITE	BLACK	WHITE	BLACK
1 P—K4	P—K4	4 B—N5	B—N5
2 N—KB3	N—QB3	5 Castles	Castles
3 N—B3	N—B3	6 BxN	. . . .

In a game with the same opening (page 57) Black played 6 . . . NPxB? This led to lasting difficulties for him because of the Queen Bishop's inability to develop. Here Black recaptures with his Queen Pawn, making it possible for the Bishop to develop effectively.

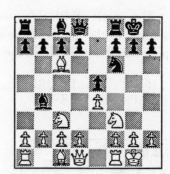

69

How should Black retake?

6	QPxB!	8 B—N5	P—KR3
7 P—Q3	B—Q3	9 B—R4	P—B4!

70

Black has set a subtle trap.

Black's last move not only prevents P—Q4; it also sets a trap into which White falls headlong.

10 N—Q5?	P—KN4!	11 NxNch	....

Likewise after 11 B—N3, NxN; 12 PxN, B—N5 Black has all the play.

11	QxN	14 QxB	QxQ
12 B—N3	B—N5!	15 PxQ	P—KB3
13 P—KR3	BxN	16 K—N2	....

How to Seize the Initiative • 91

The result of Black's positional trap is that he is in effect a piece to the good. White's Bishop is a dead piece, and can play no effective role in the game.

| 16 .... | P—QR4 | 18 R—R1 | K—K3 |
| 17 P—QR4 | K—B2 | 19 P—R4 | KR—QN1 |

71

Black is a piece ahead!

Black's strategy is delightfully simple. He plays to open a file on the Queen-side, by advancing ... P—N4 and ... P—B5. Then his "extra" piece is bound to win for him.

| 20 PxP | RPxP | 22 R—QR2 | P—N4 |
| 21 P—N3 | P—B3 | 23 KR—R1 | P—B5 |

If now 24 NPxP Black wins easily after 24 ... PxBP; 25 PxP, R—N5 etc.

24 RPxP	PxP/N6	27 P—Q4	R—N4
25 BPxP	RxP	28 R—B4	R—N5
26 R—R4	RxP	29 RxBP	RxP

White resigns, as he is powerless against Black's "extra" piece. There is a great deal to be learned from the way Black seized the initiative by taking advantage of White's careless 10th move.

Lost initiative by an error of judgment

In the following game Black sees his opportunity to seize the initiative when White condemns his King Bishop to lasting inactivity. Then Black continues to exercise cumulative pressure on White's weakened position.

SICILIAN DEFENSE

WHITE	BLACK		WHITE	BLACK
1 P—K4	P—QB4		6 B—K2	P—K4
2 N—KB3	P—Q3		7 N—N3	B—K3
3 P—Q4	PxP		8 Castles	QN—Q2
4 NxP	N—KB3		9 P—B4	Q—B2
5 N—QB3	P—QR3		10 P—B5?	....

72

Black can now take the initiative.

With Pawns on the white squares King 4 and King Bishop 5, White has reduced the mobility of his King Bishop to an alarming extent. If this piece is not "dead," it is certainly "half-dead." Another drawback to White's last move is that it releases pressure on the center, thereby enabling Black to react eventually with . . . P—Q4!

10	B—B5		13 Q—K2	QR—B1
11 B—Q3	P—QN4!		14 QR—B1	Castles
12 B—K3	B—K2		15 N—Q2	P—Q4!

How to Seize the Initiative • 93

Declaration of independence. As in the previous game, White's colorless opening has been the first step in Black's seizure of the initiative.

True, Black permits White to get rid of the useless Bishop and cancel Black's pressure on the half-open Queen Bishop file. But Black exacts a heavy price: the opening of the Queen file for Black's forces.

16 BxB	QPxB	18 PxP	BxP
17 P—QR3	P—N5!	19 P—N4	. . . .

A gesture toward attack on the King-side. But Black is well prepared for it. The permanent result is a weakness that Black will exploit later on.

19	BxN	23 K—R1	KR—Q1
20 PxB	Q—B3!	24 Q—K2	P—R3
21 Q—N2	N—B4!	25 R—R1	Q—Q3
22 BxN	QxBch	26 KR—Q1	. . . .

73

Black is ready for the final blow.

26 . . . .   Q—B3!

Black threatens 27 . . . RxN!; 28 RxR, NxKP and wins because of the menace of a murderous discovered check.

If now 27 R—KN1, RxN!; 28 QxR, NxKP; 29 Q—N2, N—B7 mate. Or if 27 R—K1, NxNP! winning a Pawn.

| 27 K—N2 | R—Q3! | | 29 K—B3 | Q—Q2! |
| 28 P—R3 | QR—Q1! | | 30 K—K3 | .... |

74

How does Black add the last bit of pressure that topples White's position?

White has rushed in his King to the center to bolster his position. But Black's mighty pin on the Queen file leaves White helpless while the Black Knight makes a lengthy trip to Queen Knight 4.

| 30 .... | N—K1! | | 32 RxKP | N—N4! |
| 31 R—R5 | N—B2! | | 33 R—Q5 | .... |

Losing the Exchange by 33 RxN is even worse.

| 33 .... | RxR | | 35 Q—B3 | NxRch |
| 34 PxR | NxP | | Resigns | |

White has no compensation for the loss of the Exchange. Having seized the initiative at an early stage, Black made admirable use of it thereafter.

Thus, in all the games in this chapter, we have seen the various ways that Black can seize the initiative in consequence of faulty play by White.

Chapter Nine

HOW TO PLAY AGAINST GAMBITS

TO KNOW how to refute a gambit is one of the most important qualifications for playing the Black pieces skillfully.

Gambits are among the most critical tests that confront you as a chessplayer.

Gambits are those openings in which Black quickly receives some material "on spec" because White hopes to bewilder or terrify him.

Some players, when they meet a gambit, put up only token resistance. Others fight back sturdily. What produces defeat in one case, and victory in another?

To succeed against a gambit, you must keep two valuable principles in mind:

(1) In a gambit, the *initiative* is much more important than material advantage. Aim cold-bloodedly and consistently for the initiative.

(2) Remember this: You can use the material advantage you have received as an excellent means of seizing the initiative. Very often the best use you can make of this material advantage is *to give back the extra material* to your opponent!

Why? Because your opponent needs a move or two to pick up the sacrificed material. If you are alert, you can make use of that time to further your development, your plans, your attack. In short, watch for a chance to seize the initiative!

Psychological warfare

You can learn a great deal from the way Black handles this game. He produces a finish which is among the most artistic ever seen in a game of chess. That alone is a broad hint that he seized the initiative at a fairly early stage.

But what is even more important is the mood in which he plays a gambit. "I'm not afraid of your gambit," he seems to tell White, "and at the same time I don't intend to put myself to a lot of trouble holding on to the Pawn. In fact, you can have it back any time you please—it's a matter of indifference to me.

"To force my pieces into a twisted, cramped position for the sake of holding onto a Pawn—that's not for me! I want to draw the sting out of your gambit and play the game *my* way.

"If you want to exchange. pieces, O.K. If you want to exchange Queens, that's O.K. And if you want to get a bad game by sticking stubbornly to your so-called 'gambit attack,' that's surely O.K."

BISHOP'S OPENING

WHITE	BLACK		WHITE	BLACK
1 P—K4	P—K4		4 P—QB3	B—B4
2 B—B4	B—B4		5 P—Q4	PxP
3 P—QN4	BxNP		6 PxP	B—N5ch!

75

Black plays to exchange pieces and ease his defensive problems.

Black has little to fear from White's gambit, which aims at a powerful center and rapid development. By offering to exchange pieces Black hopes to save time.

Of course, White can avoid an exchange by 7 K—B1. But in that case he loses the castling privilege—surely a plus for Black.

7 K—B1?	B—R4*	9 BxP	Q—K2
8 Q—R5	P—Q4!	10 B—R3	N—KB3!

A long-foreseen resource, without which things might be critical for Black.

Black well knows that 11 BxQ, NxQ; 12 B—R3 is now White's best course. But Black also knows that a gambit player never contents himself with such picayune lines. The aggressor dreams of the Grand Attack!

11 BxPch?	QxB	14 N—KB3	B—Q2
12 QxB	N—B3	15 QN—Q2	NxNch
13 Q—R4	NxKP	16 NxN	Castles(Q)

76

Black has a vastly superior position; he has smashed White's flimsy gambit attack.

---

* Black does not mind 8 BxPch, KxB; 9 Q—R5ch, P—KN3; 9 QxB, N—QB3 whereby Black gains plenty of time in exchange for the returned Pawn.

Black has a splendid development. His King is perfectly safe. White's forces are disorganized and he cannot castle his King into safety.

Black's play has been first class, psychologically as well as technically. With moves 6, 8, and 10 he has turned White's jaunty gambit into a miserable failure. From now on, Black has it all his own way.

| 17 QR—N1 | Q—Q4! | 19 R—Q1 | KR—K1! |
| 18 N—B3 | B—B4 | 20 B—B5 | .... |

Black's initiative is now so powerful that he can allow himself a beautiful Queen's sacrifice.

77

Black's Queen sacrifice will leave White defenseless.

| 20 .... | QxN!! | 22 K—N1 | R—K3 |
| 21 PxQ | B—R6ch | 23 Q—B2 | RxP! |

Another winning way is 23 . . . N—K4!

| 24 BxR | NxB |

White resigns because after 25 Q—Q3 Black mates by 25 . . . R—N3ch etc. or by 25 . . . N—K7ch etc.

Aggressive counterattack

In the next game, too, the defender proclaims very quickly that he is not interested in defending. He captures the gambit Pawn on move 2, returns a Pawn on move 4.

Black's paradoxical theory is that White's gambit move 2 P—KB4 is precisely the move that is to give *Black* a powerful attack. And that is the way that Black executes his attack, helped by White's greediness.

To appreciate this game to the full, you must bear in mind that Black is a very powerful player, while White is comparatively weak. Consequently, Black is not impressed by his adversary's choice of an aggressive opening.

From the start, Black reveals his disrespect for his opponent. The cocky 4 . . . P—QN4! tells the story. It proclaims that Black is not interested in any measly gambit Pawns.

The mere moves of this game do not tell the whole story. Black plays energetically, joyously, aggressively: he is out to win. He has no trouble crashing through White's mediocre defense.

BISHOP'S GAMBIT

WHITE	BLACK		WHITE	BLACK
1 P—K4	P—K4		4 K—B1	P—QN4!?
2 P—KB4	PxP		5 BxNP	N—KB3
3 B—B4	Q—R5ch		6 N—QB3	. . . .

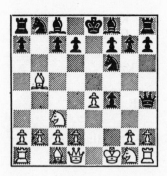

78

Black plays for a brisk attack against White's King, which has lost the castling privilege.

Black has already given notice that nothing less than monopolizing the attack will suit him. This has the psychological effect of scaring White out of the resourceful attitude he needs for coping with the attack.

| 6 .... | N—N5 | 8 N—Q5 | N—Q5! |
| 7 N—R3 | N—QB3 | 9 NxPch?* | .... |

Black's policy has succeeded. White is so confused that he misses his last chance of a proper defense.

| 9 .... | K—Q1 | 10 NxR | .... |

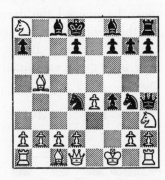

79

Black can win material or continue the attack. Which should he choose?

The simplest course for Black is 10 . . . NxB and in due course he will pick up the White Knight in the corner. This would give Black a winning material advantage, and most players would choose this safe and sane course. But Black reasons differently: he wants to win quickly and elegantly; and so he does.

| 10 .... | P—B6! | 11 P—Q3 | P—B3 |

---

* Here White misses his last chance to hold the game by 9 B—K2. Earlier, he had better moves in 6 N—KB3, driving off Black's Queen by attack, and in 7 or 8 Q—K1, disconcerting Black by offering the exchange of Queens.

Black's play here is an object-lesson for the student. His tenth move was a real battering ram, breaking up White's King-side formation no matter how White plays. Black realizes full well that White's inability to castle is an important asset for the Black attack.

Now, most are apt to get overconfident in such a situation. Not so Black. Though he is concentrating on a brilliant attack, he does not fail to provide against the threatened 12 B—N5ch winning his Queen.

12 B—QB4 P—Q4!   13 BxP   B—Q3!

Black is weaving a diabolical plot. With his sly twelfth move he opened the diagonal for his Queen Bishop. With his thirteenth move he got his other Bishop into the attack. Can you see why Black played these moves? If not, you will find them explained in the note to Black's sixteenth move.

14 Q—K1   PxPch   15 KxP   . . . .

80

Black has set the stage for a very beautiful Queen sacrifice.

15 . . . .   QxNch!!

The move that Black has been angling for.

16 KxQ   N—K6 dis ch

Now we see that Black's twelfth move made this discovered check possible.

Note also that White's K—N3 is ruled out because of Black's thirteenth move.

17 K—R4   N—B6ch   18 K—R5 B—N5 mate

Black played with true artistry and wound up with a brilliant finish.

Here is how the game would have ended after 14 P—B3: 14 . . . PxPch; 15 KxP, QxNch!!; 16 KxQ, N—K6 dis ch; 17 K—R4. Now Black has to choose a different course from the one used in the actual game:

17 . . . N—N7ch; 18 K—R5, P—N3ch; 19 K—R6, B—B1 mate!

Parrying a surprise gambit

The following game is one that needs to be studied in terms of personalities. Black is a twelve-year-old youngster who grew up to become World Champion. His opponent is an experienced, mature player who hopes to outwit the boy by adopting a complicated gambit attack.

HAMPPE-ALLGAIER GAMBIT

WHITE	BLACK	WHITE	BLACK
1 P—K4	P—K4	5 P—KR4	P—N5
2 N—QB3	N—QB3	6 N—KN5?!	P—KR3
3 P—B4	PxP	7 NxP!?	KxN
4 N—B3	P—KN4		

Black's situation is one that might well trouble a sophisticated master. His King is exposed to attack and can never castle. True, he is a piece ahead, but White can pick up some Pawns in the following play, leaving him almost equal in material.

The real difficulty for Black is that he is likely to fall badly behind in development. Apparently White has done well in choosing this tricky, complicated opening.

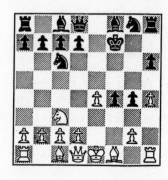

81

Black must evolve a resourceful plan.

| 8 P—Q4 | P—Q4! | 10 K—B2 | P—N6ch |
| 9 PxP | Q—K2ch! | 11 K—N1 | .... |

82

Black is about to spring a clever surprise.

A glance at Diagram 82 gives the impression that Black has virtually committed suicide. He has already lost two Pawns for the sacrificed piece, and after his attacked Knight moves he will lose a third and fourth Pawn. Worse yet, Black will be hopelessly behind in development.

11 ....   NxP!!

With this magnificent resource Black reveals that he understands very well how to free himself from an uncomfortable bind. The move is hard to see, if only because it leaves Black behind in material—though not for long.

12 QxN   Q—B4!!

Now we see the point of Black's sly countersacrifice: if 13 QxQ??, BxQch and mate next move!

13 N—K2	Q—N3!	14 QxQ	RPxQ

Black still threatens mate!

15 N—Q4	B—QB4	16 P—B3	R—R5

Black plays with remarkable ingenuity. He now threatens 17 . . . RxN!; 18 PxR, BxPch and mate follows.

If White tries 17 P—N4, then 17 . . . RxNP! smashes his defense.

Aside from these tactical details, Black has buried White's King Rook for the rest of the game.

17 B—K2	BxNch	19 P—N3	N—B3
18 PxB	RxQP	20 B—N2	R—Q7!

Of course not 20 . . . RxP?; 21 B—B4 and Black loses the Rook because of the pin.

In this situation White can avoid loss of a piece with 21 BxN, KxB; 22 B—B3. But then, with a Pawn down, he has no counterchances in the cut-and-dried endgame that would follow. So he tries a different way, but Black is ready for him.

21 B—R5ch	NxB!	22 BxR	P—B6!
	23 PxP	N—B5!	

83

The concentrated attack of Black's pieces must be decisive.

If now 24 R—K1, Black has a lovely finish with 24 . . . B—R6!; 25 B—K5, R—KN7ch; 26 K—B1, R—KB7 dbl ch; 27 K—N1, R—B8 ch!; 28 RxR, N—K7 mate!

24 B—K5	R—KN7ch	26 K—K1	N—Q6ch
25 K—B1	R—KB7ch	Resigns	

Black wins the Bishop, leaving White in a hopeless situation.

A fascinating game because of the way that Black spiked the unfamiliar gambit attack and seized the initiative. (The Black pieces were played by José Raoul Capablanca.)

Diverting the gambit attack

Though artless greed proves White's undoing in this game, Black deserves lots of credit for leading him astray. On move 3 Black is offered material, which he respectfully declines. Then, only two moves later, *he* is offering material!

Soon Black has a surprisingly powerful initiative which results in a convincing win. Above all, note how he refuses to be appeased by material gain, and always searches for the most incisive move.

WHITE	BLACK
1 P—K4	P—K4
2 N—QB3	N—KB3
3 P—B4	P—Q4

WHITE	BLACK
4 BPxP	NxP
5 Q—B3	N—QB3!

84

Black's last move reveals his intentions to counterattack.

Black plays boldly for counterattack, instead of being concerned about his doubly attacked Knight at the K5 square.

Black knows, to be sure, that 6 B—N5 is White's best reply—but he hopes that White will play 6 NxN? expecting 6 . . . NxP?? when 7 Q—KN3! wins a piece!

6 NxN?	N—Q5!	7 Q—B4	PxN

If now 8 QxKP??, B—KB4 when Black wins.

8 B—B4	B—KB4	9 P—B3!?	P—KN4!

Black is too crafty to snap at 9 . . . N—B7ch; 10 K—Q1, NxR; 11 QxB. For in that case White threatens mate, with plenty of time to pick up the wandering Black Knight afterwards.

In the event of 10 Q—B1 (in reply to Black's last move),

Black has the delightful line 10 ... N—B7ch; 11 K—Q1???, N—K6ch winning White's Queen.

10 BxPch   KxB   11 Q—B2   ....

85

Should Black play to win more material?

Again Black has the tempting . . . N—B7ch within his reach. But after 12 K—Q1, NxR; 13 QxBch, K—N2 he is bound to lose his wandering Knight and his King is somewhat exposed.

So, Black correctly reasons, he is not going to part with his initiative for such a doubtful gain. Instead, he hits hard with:

11 ....   P—K6!!

The first point of Black's sly idea is this: 12 QxP???, N—B7ch winning White's Queen!

Another fine point of Black's plan is that though he must apparently lose a piece when his Knight moves, he manages to hold on to his material advantage.

12 Q—B1   PxPch!

Black continues to find the strongest moves. If now 13

BxP, Black replies now 13 . . . N—B7ch with a decisive gain of material—even a mate in some cases.

| 13 K—Q1 | PxB/Qch | | 14 KxQ | P—N5! |

Black would not mind 15 PxN, for then he could force mate by 15 . . . B—R3ch; 16 K—Q1, QxPch etc.

| 15 P—N4 | Q—N4ch | | 16 K—Q1 | R—Q1! |

White resigns in this hopeless situation, 17 PxN, RxPch being obviously disastrous for him.

Black's brisk counterattack made mincemeat out of White's slovenly set-up.

Neutralizing White's initiative

In this game, as in the previous one, Black's initiative is the deciding factor. But the mechanics of victory are different. In the previous game Black tempted White to succumb to fatal greed; in this game White fails because he loses time in the opening.

Note, too, that Black's play here is just as consistent, just as grimly efficient, as in the previous game. But instead of spectacular play we have here Black's smooth, logical, irresistible piling up of pressure that leaves White helpless.

FALKBEER COUNTER GAMBIT

WHITE	BLACK		WHITE	BLACK
1 P—K4	P—K4		5 N—Q2	PxP
2 P—KB4	P—Q4		6 BxP	NxP
3 KPxP	P—K5		7 N—K4	N—N5!
4 P—Q3	N—KB3		8 B—N5ch	P—QB3!

Black's shrewd thrust at move 7 has given him the initiative, which cannot be taken away from him even by the simplifying exchange of Queens.

86

Despite the coming exchange of Queens, Black already has his opponent on the defensive.

White's game is already in need of vitamins. Certainly there is no chance for the dashing kind of play White seeks when he plays a gambit.

9	QxQch	KxQ	12	K—Q1	P—B3
10	B—R4	B—KB4	13	N/N5—B3	N/N1—R3!
11	N—N5	K—K1			

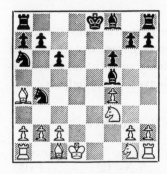

87

Black's position gathers power from move to move.

Thanks to Black's forceful play, White's original lead in development has evaporated and his pieces are awkwardly placed.

With skillful change of pace Black has alternated between

attacking and developing moves. He is now ready for . . .
N—B4 and also . . . R—Q1ch. These moves will increase his
positional advantage.

14	P—QR3	R—Q1ch	17	B—N3	NxB
15	B—Q2	N—Q4	18	PxN	B—Q3
16	K—K2	N—B4			

Black keeps hammering away at White's game. Now that
Black has two Bishops against Bishop and Knight, he pro-
ceeds to use the Bishops to press down all the harder on
White's position.

| 19 | P—N3 | K—B2 | 21 | K—B2 | B—N3ch |
| 20 | R—QB1 | B—B2 | 22 | K—N2 | KR—K1 |

88

*Note how Black's Bishops have be-
come stronger.*

Black has all his pieces in magnificent play and continues
to pile on the pressure relentlessly. White, on the other
hand, is still unable to develop his King Knight and King
Rook at this late date.

Now Black continues in the same forceful style to wind
up with a crushing finish.

How to Play against Gambits • 111

23	P—R3	N—K6ch		26	B—B3	N—Q8
24	K—R2	R—Q6		27	P—N4	B—K5
25	P—QN4	R/K1—Q1		28	N—K1	....

89

Black must come out at least a piece ahead.

| | | |
| 28 | .... | R—Q7ch! |

Resigns

After 29 BxR, RxBch Black wins pretty much as he pleases.

The moral we derive from all these games is that in gambits, the initiative matters most of all. What we have seen in this chapter is that Black is most likely to succeed when he spots the factors that will give him the initiative; when he fights consistently for these advantages; and when he hits hard, once he has achieved those advantages.

These are the ways in which Black successfully hammers away at gambits.

Chapter Ten

HOW TO DEFEND AGAINST A
POWERFUL ATTACK

A FAMOUS English philosopher once wrote, "He is happy whose circumstances suit his temper; but he is more excellent who can suit his temper to any circumstance."

So it is with chessplayers. They love the attack above all; they want to attack at all times, and at all costs. But this kind of chess is akin to an exclusive diet of nesselrode pie.

Chess positions are of all kinds, and we cannot always choose what kind of game we are going to have. If we dislike certain types of positions, our gleeful opponents will be sure to inflict them on us.

Defensive ability is an important quality in chessplayers, and one that will give satisfaction and win many points. Besides, though some of us may flinch from defensive tasks, we really have the determination and perseverance to fight through to victory in a defensive position.

Of course, at some point or other a well-conducted defense must take the form of dynamic counterattack, or even outright attack. This is the reward and even the duty of good defensive play. The following examples show you how it's done.

Maneuvering in a crowded position

Crowded positions are undesirable because your pieces cannot operate to the best advantage. A great master was fond of saying that "crowded positions carry within themselves the germ of defeat." By this he meant that a player afflicted with a cramped position would gradually be pushed to the wall.

The best way to handle a crowded position is to avoid it. But all the best principles and maxims in the world cannot save us from sometimes getting into unfavorable or difficult situations.

If your pieces are in a crowded position, you must always be on the lookout for opportunities to free yourself. This is easier said than done, for you may look and look for many moves, while the opportunity for freedom may come at only one point and may be rather hidden at that.

Nevertheless the advice is valuable: *watch for a chance to free yourself.* To be aware of the difficulty and to be determined to solve it, is often half the battle. If you can figure out the freeing method in advance, that is a great help.

Here is a useful hint, illustrated in the following game: *the thrust for freedom will generally come in the center.*

OLD-INDIAN DEFENSE

WHITE	BLACK		WHITE	BLACK
1 P—Q4	N—KB3		5 P—K4	B—K2
2 P—QB4	P—Q3		6 B—Q3	Castles
3 N—KB3	QN—Q2		7 Castles	PxP!?
4 N—B3	P—K4		8 NxP	R—K1

Black "surrendered the center" on move 7. He now has no Pawn on his fourth rank, while White has two Pawns on *his* fourth rank.

The result is White's Pawns control more center squares

than Black's Pawns do. Black's pieces have less maneuvering space in the center than White's pieces do.

9 P—QN3	N—K4		12 P—KR3	B—KB1
10 B—B2	P—QR3		13 P—B4	N—N3
11 B—N2	B—Q2			

90

Black must now maneuver ingeniously in the center.

Black's position looks uncomfortably cramped, but he has his compensations. By attacking White's King Pawn, he limits White's freedom of action. Also, Black is well posted to prevent the aggressive advance P—K5.

But Black has other ideas. His main idea is to free himself some time later by . . . P—Q4. First he must play . . . P—B3 to make that move possible. Second, he must play . . . P—Q4 at a time when the powerful reply P—K5 is not feasible.

The later course of the game will show how Black carries out his idea.

14 Q—B3	P—B3!		16 Q—Q3	Q—B2
15 QR—K1	P—N4!		17 K—R1	....

Black's judgment has been vindicated. White's development looks very impressive, but with P—K5 or P—KB5 ruled out, Black has little to fear.

(Why is P—KB5 ruled out? Because the move allows . . . N—K4, giving one of the Black Knights a magnificent and unassailable center post.)

| 17 .... | QR—Q1 | 18 B—N1 | P—N5! |

91

Black is gradually freeing his position.

Black has made considerable progress. By driving off White's Queen Knight, he brings himself an important step nearer to playing . . . P—Q4. (White will now have one piece less bearing down on the important Queen 5 square.)

Black has scored another point as well. By making White's P—QN4 impossible, he is able to establish a Black Knight at his Queen Bishop 4 square. From that point the Knight will bear down strongly on the center.

| 19 N—Q1 | B—B1! | 21 N—B5 | N—B4! |
| 20 Q—KB3 | N—Q2! | 22 P—N4? | N—K3! |

Alertly taking advantage of White's weakening 22nd move, Black attacks the King Bishop Pawn and prepares for the final freeing maneuver.

| 23 Q—N3 | B—N2! | 24 P—KR4 | P—Q4!! |

92

Black has freed his game!

At just the ideal moment, and with the maximum amount of impact, Black has freed his game.

Note that . . . P—Q4!! is very strong because it opens up the diagonal leading to White's King. Consequently this brings Black's cooped-up Bishop at the Queen Knight 2 square into powerful play.

Note, also, that Black gains time by playing . . . P—Q4!! since he is attacking White's King Bishop Pawn.

Note, finally, that White's reaction of P—K5 loses all impact because of Black's grip on the long diagonal.

| 25 P—K5 | P—B4! | 26 PxP | RxP |

Now that the diagonal of his Bishop at Queen Knight 2 is fully open, Black threatens all sorts of brutal discovered checks, such as . . . RxN dis ch or . . . R—Q6 dis ch.

Black has arranged matters so cunningly that he can answer 27 B—K4 with 27 . . . RxN! and wins.

| 27 K—N1 | R—Q7! | 28 N/B5—K3 | .... |

Something had to be done about the threat of . . . R—N7ch. (In the event of 28 R—B2, Black has a winning reply in 28 . . . R/K1—Q1.)

But Black's next move (menacing . . . Q—R8 mate!) forces White's surrender.

| 28 .... | Q—B3! | 29 R—B3 | QxR |

White resigns. Black's skillful maneuvering in his crowded position was extremely impressive. He knew he had to free his game and he knew how to go about it.

Defense by counterattack

When you play the Black pieces, you are frequently called upon to make a sharp, accurate appraisal of what your opponent is aiming for.

We more or less take it for granted that White has the birthright of the attack, and that he is entitled to the initiative. However, there is no guarantee that White's judgment is always sound, and that his execution of the attack is always impeccable.

As player of the Black pieces, it is your job to assess the position; decide how much stress it can stand; coolly weigh the likely success or failure of White's efforts. If you conclude that the attack will be insufficient, you can look for counterattack.

Should you decide that White's efforts on the King-side are unlikely to succeed, you can counterattack on the other side of the board. Such Queen-side counterattacks are quite common. In the following game Black carries out this plan with commendable skill.

QUEEN'S GAMBIT DECLINED

WHITE	BLACK	WHITE	BLACK
1 P—Q4	P—Q4	5 P—K3	QN—Q2
2 P—QB4	P—K3	6 B—Q3	PxP
3 N—KB3	N—KB3	7 BxBP	P—QN4
4 N—B3	P—B3	8 B—Q3	P—QR3

Black's Queen Bishop is blocked by his Pawn at King 3. His last three moves have been directed toward opening a new, clear diagonal for the Bishop. Black needs one more move (. . . P—B4!) to achieve this objective.

9 N—K4*	P—B4!	11 NxQN	BxN
10 PxP?	NxP	12 Castles	B—N2

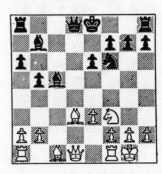

93

Black is ahead in development!

How did Black obtain his lead in development? He took advantage of White's faulty maneuver in moving his Queen Knight three times—only to exchange it off. White's 10th move was another time-waster, aiding Black's development.

White ought to take a very modest view of this situation. Instead, he strives for attack.

Is Black impressed? Not at all. With his lead in development and perfectly solid King-side position, he need not fear any coming attack.

13 P—QN3	Castles	15 R—B1	QR—B1
14 B—N2	Q—K2	16 Q—K2	B—R6!

---

* White's most forceful line is 9 P—K4, P—B4; 10 P—K5, PxP; 11 NxNP with a complicated game.

Black intends to concentrate on the Queen-side. By removing White's protective Queen Bishop he will be able to play . . . N—Q4 and . . . N—B6, planting the Knight with great effect in White's position.

17 KR—Q1	N—Q4!		19 QxB	P—N5!
18 B—N1	BxB		20 Q—K5	N—B6!

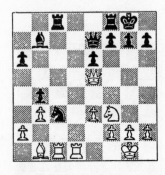

94

Black has achieved his objective on the Queen-side.

Black has a won game, for if now 21 R—Q2 or 21 R—K1, he plays 21 . . . N—K7ch! with decisive effect. White must therefore carry out the attack he has been plotting for some time.

21 RxN	PxR!		23 Q—R5ch	K—N1
22 BxPch	KxB		24 N—N5	....

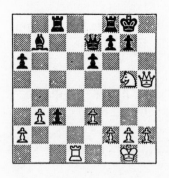

95

Black is threatened with mate on the move.

Black must do something about the threat of 25 Q—R7 mate.

$$24 \ldots \quad \text{B—K5!!}$$

This nonsensical-looking move is actually a brilliant resource that gains a priceless tempo. (After White's reply he will no longer threaten mate!)

25 NxB	P—B7	26 R—QB1	KR—Q1!

Black avoids a sly trap here: if 26 . . . Q—R6?; 27 N—B6ch!, PxN; 28 Q—N4ch and White forces a perpetual check!

$$27 \ \text{P—KR3} \quad \ldots.$$

On 27 P—KR4 Black planned 27 . . . Q—R6; 28 N—N5, QxRch; 29 K—R2, R—B2 and White has nothing: 30 Q—R7ch, K—B1; 31 Q—R8ch, K—K2. Black is then safe, with an overwhelming material advantage.

(Black could win by the same line after the move actually played by White; but he prefers a different, prettier line.)

27	P—B4	29 QxQ	R—Q8ch
28 N—N5	QxN!	30 K—R2	....

Here we have the point of Black's Queen sacrifice. If 30 RxR, PxR/Qch and Black is a Rook ahead.

$$30 \ldots. \quad \text{RxR}$$

White resigns. A masterly effort by Black. He appraised the situation correctly; this led him to start a Queen-side demonstration which soon showed up the futility of White's efforts.

How to Defend against a Powerful Attack • 121

Note that Black's Queen-side demonstration resulted in the passed Pawn which eventually won the game for Black!

Defending against a violent attack

Very often a chessplayer is called upon to defend himself against a violent attack. In the nature of things, Black is generally the player who has to do the defending.

For most of us, defense is an irksome chore. It requires lasting attention; it puts you under great strain; it gives you the double task of not only foreseeing your future defensive resources, but foreseeing your opponent's future attacking resources!

However, good defensive play is highly rewarding. So few players have mastered it that possessing this skill puts you ahead of your opponents. Good defensive play salvages many a game that is really lost or one that only looks lost.

Too many players forget that attack is only a part of chess, and that we cannot always have the kind of positions we like. If you have patience and faith in the resisting power of defensive positions, you will win many more games.

The following example shows what can be done to hold the fort against an attack which is persistent, forceful, and inventive.

BISHOP'S GAMBIT

WHITE	BLACK	WHITE	BLACK
1 P—K4	P—K4	5 N—QB3	Q—K2
2 P—KB4	PxP	6 P—Q4	N—B3
3 B—B4	N—K2	7 N—B3	Q—N5
4 Q—R5	N—N3	8 Q—Q5	N—Q1

As you can see, Black is very tenacious. He has captured the gambit Pawn on move 2, and he means to hold on to it no matter what difficulties may arise to plague him.

This type of defense against a gambit is not recommended in Chapter 3; but it is precisely this kind of stubbornness that will lead to a very cramped game for Black—the kind of position we want to study at this point.

| 9 P—QR3 | Q—K2 | 11 Q—KR5 | P—QB3 |
| 10 Castles | P—Q3 | 12 B—Q2 | .... |

96

Black plans to castle on the Queen-side.

Black is far behind in development, and he must plan to get his King into safety before White finds some violent method to open up the center lines.

Black therefore gets the idea of preparing for Queen-side castling. However, White spoils this plan.

| 12 .... | N—K3 | 13 QR—K1! | Q—B2! |

Black realizes that his plan won't work: if 13 ... B—Q2; 14 P—Q5!, N—B2; 15 PxP, PxP and his Queen-side is too exposed for castling there.

| 14 P—Q5 | N—Q1 | 15 P—K5 | .... |

(See diagram on top of next page)

97

Black's position looks lost!

It would seem that Black cannot defend his King against White's vigorous onslaught in the center. Most players would give up hope here, but Black has just begun to fight.

15	QPxP!	17 K—R1	Castles
16 NxP	B—B4ch!	18 PxP	....

The way Black saved himself from disaster by finding a way to castle verges on the miraculous!

But he is by no means out of danger. For example, if now 18 . . . PxP?; 19 NxN, RPxN; 20 QxB and White has won a piece.

However, Black finds a magnificent counterstroke in this critical situation:

$$18 ....\qquad B—K6!!$$

Attacking White's undefended Bishop. If now 19 BxB (the natural reply), QxN! and no matter how White plays, he loses a piece! For example, 20 QxQ, NxQ and both White Bishops are attacked.

The consequence is that White decides to sacrifice a piece to keep the attack boiling at full force. True, Black's position is still full of hazard, but now White has to take chances too.

19 N—B3   BxB!

With this move Black gives his opponent an unpleasant choice. If now 20 NxB, PxP and White's attack has petered out ingloriously, with Black triumphantly clutching his extra (gambit) Pawn.

So, White decides to sacrifice a piece—a psychological victory for Black.

20 N—KN5!   P—KR3

The only reply to White's threat of mate on the move.

21 QxN   PxN   22 N—Q5!   ....

Attacking Black's Queen and also threatening 23 N—B6ch, K—R1; 24 Q—R7 mate. But even in this crisis Black finds a way out.

22 ....   QxP!

Black is not afraid of the following forking check!*

23 N—K7ch   K—R1

98

Black is still holding his own!

---

* Black can escape by 22 . . . PxQ; 23 NxQ dis ch, K—R2; 24 NxR, BxR; but he prefers to fight it out in the hardest variation.

How to Defend against a Powerful Attack • 125

Black's resourceful defense holds in every line.

Thus if 24 NxQ, PxQ and he remains a piece ahead.

Or 24 Q—R5ch, Q—KR3 with the same result.

Finally—and this was the crucial variation calculated by Black—if 24 BxP, NxB!; 25 NxQ, BxR; 26 N—K7!, B—Q7; 27 Q—R5ch, N—R3; 28 N—N6ch, K—N1; 29 NxR, KxN and Black's material advantage of three minor pieces against the Queen should win the game for him.

| 24 QxP/N5 | Q—KR3! | 25 Q—QB5 | N—K3 |

Directed against the threat of 26 N—N6ch. White is still making attacking gestures, but Black has the game well in hand.

| 26 BxN | BxB | 27 R—K5 | B—K6! |

White was threatening to win Black's Queen with R—R5. But now Black is ready to seize the attack.

99

Black has survived the storm of attacking threats.

| 28 Q—N5 | P—KN3! | 29 QxP | K—N2 |

Now the initiative is in Black's hands. He threatens 30 . . . QxPch!!; 31 KxQ, R—R1ch and mate next move.

30 Q—B3	QR—Q1	33 QxQB	QxQ
31 P—R3	Q—R5	34 PxQ	R—R1ch
32 N—B6	B—N5!	35 R—KR5	PxR

White resigns.

This game, a masterpiece of superb defensive play, shows what can be accomplished by tenacious and ingenious defense. Few games will ever call for such difficult maneuvering in the face of so powerful an attack.

The King as a fighting piece

The most important of all our defensive jobs is protecting the King from harm. Though most players err on the side of neglecting this task, they sometimes go to the other extreme and become too cautious.

There are times when firmness and daring are called for —times when routine caution is not good enough. In the following extraordinary game, Black is well aware of the need for bold handling of his King.

CARO-KANN DEFENSE

WHITE	BLACK	WHITE	BLACK
1 P—K4	P—QB3	5 B—KB4	N—B3
2 P—Q4	P—Q4	6 N— Q2	P—KN3
3 PxP	PxP	7 KN—B3	B—N2
4 P—QB3	N—QB3	8 P—KR3	N—K5

An adventurous move which leads to a very difficult game for Black.

| 9 NxN | PxN | 10 N—Q2 | P—B4 |

The only practicable way to guard the King Pawn; but after White's reply Black will be unable to castle.

11 B—B4! . . . .

100

Black is unable to castle.

As the position now stands, Black cannot get his King into a safe position and he cannot post his Rooks for rapid action.

True, Black has a makeshift solution in 11 . . . P—K3, which makes castling possible. But then the Pawn at King 3 is a lasting weakness—always under attack by White's King Bishop. Worse yet, Black's Queen Bishop is then a permanent prisoner.

Black therefore comes to a courageous and highly unconventional decision:

11	P—K4!!	12 PxP	NxP

This Knight has to be captured, as Black threatens . . . NxB or . . . N—Q6ch; with a fine game in either case.

13 BxN	BxB	14 Q—N3	Q—N3!

Naturally Black offers the exchange of Queens, for then all danger to his King will vanish.

101

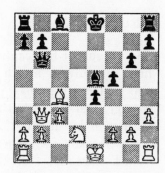

Black's King is ready to embark on a long tour.

15 B—N5ch	K—K2!	18 Castles(Q)	B—K3
16 N—B4	Q—B4	19 B—B4	BxB
17 NxB	QxN	20 QxB	KR—Q1!

102

Black's King is about to advance fearlessly.

Black's last move is a daring one; his King is about to end up well in the opponent's camp. The brilliant originality of Black's plan is that he foresees that his King, paradoxically enough, will be quite safe.

21 Q—N4ch   K—B3!!

The only correct move. Black realizes that if his King goes to King Bishop 2, his Queen Knight Pawn is lost with check. If his King goes to King 1, White plays QxNP threatening QxKRP followed by QxNPch.

How to Defend against a Powerful Attack • 129

22 QxNP   Q—B5ch   23 K—N1   QxP

As a result of this capture, Black has a passed King Pawn which is ready to march down to the queening square as soon as the storm has passed. This means, in technical language, that White has a lost endgame in prospect unless he can win by attack. Consequently, the safety of Black's King is the key factor in the following play.

Black does not fear´ 24 QxKRP, for his King Knight Pawn is guarded, thanks to his 21st move. Furthermore, if 24 QxKRP, Black replies 24 . . . QxKNP, with *two connected passed Pawns*—an overwhelming positional advantage. So White tries a different way.

24 Q—B6ch   K—N4!   25 P—R4ch K—N5!!

Black's King, as a fighting piece, heads for White's King-side Pawns. There is now a possibility that Black's King will be able later on to attack White's Pawns (. . . K—N6 etc.).

103

Black's King is attacking!

26 QR—KB1 Q—N3!

Offering the exchange of Queens; this is about the same

as inviting White to commit suicide. White's reply threatens
28 Q—K2ch and 29 R—R3 mate!

27 Q—B4   R—Q7!

Black parries the mating threat and menaces mate on
his own. Black now wins easily by stepping up the pressure.

28 P—N4	Q—K6		31 R—B4ch	K—N6!
29 R—R3	Q—N3		32 Q—Q5	R—QB1
30 R/R3—B3	RxNP		33 Q—Q7	Q—R3

White resigns. (If 34 P—R4, Q—B5.) One of the most
original games ever played, and one of the finest examples
of cool, resourceful chess under very trying circumstances.

Recovery from a lost position

So far we have seen some very fine play by Black. In
actual practice, of course, his play is not always very fine.
Often, indeed, he plays badly and finds himself with a lost
game. Yet he must not give up in despair after such poor
play, for there is often a possibility of redeeming the most
disastrous situations. And, as far as the score table is concerned, a botched game that is resourcefully salvaged is
worth just as much as a masterpiece.

KING'S INDIAN DEFENSE

WHITE	BLACK		WHITE	BLACK
1 P—Q4	N—KB3		5 N—B3	Castles
2 P—QB4	P—KN3		6 B—K2	P—K4
3 N—QB3	B—N2		7 Castles	PxP
4 P—K4	P—Q3		8 NxP	R—K1

Black has exchanged Pawns early in order to provide a
long, free diagonal for his fianchettoed Bishop. This ex-

change is questionable, however, as White's pieces obtain great freedom of action.

With his 10th move (. . . P—B3) Black weakens his Queen Pawn. His intentions, to be sure, are of the best: he wants to make room for the Queen so that he can assure communication between his Rooks.

9 P—B3	QN—Q2		12 B—K3	Q—B2
10 B—N5	P—B3		13 QR—B1	N—N3
11 Q—Q2	Q—N3		14 KR—Q1	KN—Q2

As we anticipated, Black finds his position cramped. He is not clear about what he wants or what he can achieve, and his maneuvering and regrouping is not getting him very far. His last move gives White the opportunity for a very promising attack.

104

Black has overlooked White's combination.

15 N/Q4—N5! . . . .

This is the move that Black failed to foresee.

15	PxN	16 NxP	Q—Q1

Black is on the run now.

17 NxQP   N—K4

To retreat 17 . . . R—B1 allows White to recover his piece (with a Pawn plus) by 18 NxB, RxN; 19 P—B5 etc.

| 18 P—B5! N/N3—Q2 | 19 P—B6? | . . . . |

The correct course—the one that Black feared—was 19 P—B4, N—QB3; 20 B—QB4. In that case Black has a Knight for two Pawns but he can hardly move a piece. This course would have been fatal for him.

In playing as he does, White seeks to regain the sacrificed piece. He succeeds—but only on Black's terms.

| 19 . . . . | NxQBP! |

Black finds the best move.

Note that 19 . . . PxP?? would be ruinous after 20 NxR, QxN; 21 P—B4 etc.

| 20 NxB | RxN | 21 QxN | . . . . |

White has regained his piece, but now comes Black's stunning refutation.

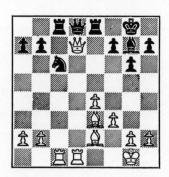

105

How does Black save the game?

| 21 . . . . | B—Q5!! |

A masterstroke. If 22 QxQ, BxBch wins a piece for Black.

And if 22 BxB? White loses his Queen.

22 RxB   NxR

Now White's best is 23 QxQ, NxBch; 24 K—B2, KRxQ when Black will win nevertheless with the Exchange for a Pawn. However, White goes to pieces:

23 B—QN5?	RxRch	25 BxQ	R—Q1!
24 BxR	QxQ	Resigns	

For after the Bishop leaves the Queen 7 square, Black wins the other Bishop by . . . N—K7ch.

Black's resilience in a very difficult situation is in striking contrast to White's tragic collapse.

The games in this chapter have highlighted the cold-blooded resourcefulness that Black must bring to difficult defensive situations. Such positions are quite trying; but, by virtue of their very difficulty, they present a challenge that is worth meeting and worth surmounting.

Chapter Eleven

HOW TO SEIZE THE ATTACK

SO FAR WE have seen how Black defends, how he reacts
to gambits, how he seizes the initiative, how he counterattacks. Now we want to see situations in which a serious
flaw in White's game gives Black a chance for a slashing
all-out attack.

One word of warning: when playing the Black pieces, do
not embark lightly on an attacking policy. Note in each of
the following games that White compromises his game in
some fashion, while Black maintains an impeccable position.

Exploiting White's faulty development

VIENNA GAME

WHITE	BLACK
1 P—K4	P—K4
2 N—QB3	N—KB3

WHITE	BLACK
3 P—B4	P—Q4
4 BPxP	NxP

106

*Black's Knight is splendidly cen-
tralized.*

5 N—B3   N—QB3   6 B—Q3?   P—KB4

White cannot very well play BxN now, as he would lose further time—and his King Pawn as well. He therefore captures Black's King Bishop Pawn in passing. This returns Black's King Knight to the King Bishop 3 square. But meanwhile White's Queen Pawn cannot advance. The result: at the end of the game, White's Queen Bishop and Queen Rook are still on their original squares.

7 PxP e.p.   NxBP   8 Castles   B—B4ch

Development with gain of time. Note that White is unable to reply P—Q4.

9 K—R1   Castles   10 B—N5   N—KN5!

Threatening to win the Exchange by . . . N—B7ch.

If White tries 11 P—Q4, then 11 . . . NxQP; 12 NxN, RxRch; 13 QxR, BxN and Black is a Pawn ahead.

Thus Black wrests another concession from White: giving up his developed Bishop, White increases Black's lead in development and his attacking prospects.

11 BxN   PxB   12 P—Q4   B—Q3

Black's attack has become very powerful; he threatens to win the Exchange by . . . B—R3.

13 P—KR3   B—R3!!

107

Can Black afford to ignore the attack on his Knight?

| 14 PxN | BxR | 15 QxB | RxN!! |

With this sacrifice, Black establishes the soundness of his previous sacrifice. First point: if 16 PxR, Black has a quick mate with 16 . . . Q—R5ch etc.

Second point: if 16 QxR, Q—R5ch—and now if 17 Q—R3, Q—K8 mate. Or 17 K—N1, Q—K8ch; 18 Q—B1, B—R7ch winning White's Queen.

But the best is yet to come.

| 16 Q—K1 | Q—R5ch!! | 17 QxQ | R—B8 mate |

Thus we see that Black's brilliant attack succeeded because White's Queen Bishop remained at home.

Exploiting White's neglected development

This game is a joy to play over because Black never misses a chance to find an energetic move. His play is forceful but not brash. White, on the other hand, dawdles. First he hits out aimlessly—and then strikes at the wrong target.

SCOTCH GAMBIT

WHITE	BLACK	WHITE	BLACK
1 P—K4	P—K4	3 P—Q4	PxP
2 N—KB3	N—QB3	4 B—QB4	N—B3

Ignoring the defense of his Queen Pawn, Black strikes at White's King Pawn.

| 5 P—K5 | . . . . |

White, too, intends to attack.

108

How does Black save his Knight?

5 ....   P—Q4!

Instead of defending, Black attacks!—and opens up the diagonal of his Queen Bishop at the same time.

6 B—QN5	N—K5	8 NxN	PxN
7 NxP	B—Q2	9 B—Q3	B—QB4

Black's obvious eagerness to attack is perfectly well grounded in the fact that he has two extra pieces in play.

10 BxN   ....

109

Should Black recapture?

10 ....   Q—R5!

The alternative 10 . . . PxB is quite satisfactory, but Black's Queen move brings still another piece into play—threatening mate, by the way.

11 Q—K2   PxB   12 B—K3   B—KN5!

Forcing a crisis, for if 13 Q—Q2 Black leaves his opponent without an adequate reply by playing 13 . . . R—Q1.

                 13 Q—B4   . . . .

Apparently crushing: if Black moves his attacked Bishop, the Queen fork 14 QxQBPch seems deadly.

                 13 . . . .   BxB!

110

Black has started a crisp winning combination.

On 14 QxQBPch Black intends 14 . . . B—Q2!!; 15 QxRch, K—K2!!; 16 QxR and Black forces mate beginning with 16 . . . QxBPch.

Suppose, however, White interpolates 16 P—KN3 in this variation? Then Black wins with 16 . . . BxPch!; 17 KxB, P—K6ch! If now 18 KxP, Q—N4ch wins White's Queen, and if 18 K—N1, P—K7! decides.

Finally, if 18 K—K1, Q—QN5ch; 19 P—B3, QxNP; 20 QxR, B—N5! and Black forces mate.

| 14 P—KN3 | Q—Q1!! | 16 K—B2 | Q—B6ch |
| 15 PxB | Q—Q8ch | 17 K—N1 | .... |

On 17 K—K1 Black had 17 . . . QxKPch; 18 K—B1, B—R6 mate.

| 17 .... | B—R6! | 19 QxRch | K—K2 |
| 18 QxQBPch | K—B1 | Resigns | |

White's Queen is *en prise* (exposed to capture) and he cannot stop mate. Beautiful play by Black.

Exploiting White's faulty plan

Sometimes White gets a good development and then embarks on a faulty plan. It takes a sharp eye to see the flaw in White's procedure. In the following delightful game Black takes admirable advantage of White's shortcomings.

GIUOCO PIANO

WHITE	BLACK	WHITE	BLACK
1 P—K4	P—K4	3 B—B4	B—B4
2 N—KB3	N—QB3	4 P—B3	....

111

Black must decide on his policy in the center.

White intends to play P—Q4. Then, if Black exchanges Pawns, White gets a powerful Pawn center and an ideal development. Black therefore determines to avoid the exchange of Pawns.

4	P—Q3	9 R—K1	Castles
5 Castles	B—N3!	10 P—QN4	K—R1!
6 P—Q4	Q—K2	11 B—R3	N—KN1!
7 P—QR4	P—QR3	12 P—N5	N—R4!
8 P—R3	N—B3	13 NxP	....

Since . . . PxN??? would lose the Queen, Black seems to have blundered. How does he regain his Pawn?

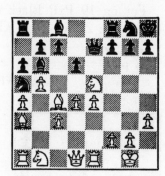

112

Black seizes the attack.

13 .... P—KB3!

With this powerful reply Black completely turns the tables. If the attacked Knight moves, Black wins a piece. Thus he forces White's reply.

14 BxN	BPxN!	15 B—R2	KPxP

If now 16 BPxP, Q—B3 is much in Black's favor.

16 N—Q2 BxP!

How to Seize the Attack • 141

113

Black's surprise sacrifice is only the beginning.

On 17 PxB Black intends 17 . . . Q—N4ch; 18 K—B1, RxPch!!; 19 KxR, P—Q6 dis ch with a crushing attack.

| 17 N—B3 | B—N5 | 18 BPxP | PxP! |

For on 19 PxP Black continues 19 . . . BxN; 20 PxB, Q—N4ch; 21 K—B1, QxPch and is ahead in material.

19 Q—Q3	BxN	21 K—B1	N—B5!
20 PxB	Q—N4ch	22 B—B1	Q—R4
	23 PxP	RxP!!	

114

Black has given his opponent another unpleasant surprise.

The point of Black's last sacrifice is that if 24 QxN, Black wins with 24 . . . R—KR6!

| 24 BxN | RxR! | 25 Q—Q1 | RxB! |

White resigns, for if QxR/B1, R—KR6! wins.

Chapter Twelve

HOW TO EXPLOIT UNUSUAL OPENINGS

In Chapter Seven we saw how dangerous it is for Black to experiment with unusual defenses which have the drawback of neglecting the center. This faulty strategy is likewise not to be recommended for White, although it involves less danger for him.

What makes the inferior openings somewhat more playable for White is that since he has the first move he may have time to avoid immediate disaster; for example, he can castle sooner and get his King into relative safety. At best, however, White will have forfeited any chance of initiative; Black's problem will be, not how to equalize, but how to exploit the oportunity offered him by White's inferior play.

The King Fianchetto

In modern play we often encounter the fianchetto deployment of a Bishop. Consequently it may seem attractive to start the game with 1 P—KN3, especially as Black may be puzzled as to the proper reply to this unusual move.

However, 1 P—KN3 has the familiar drawbacks we noticed earlier: it gives Black a free hand in the center and allows him to develop his pieces freely and efficiently. After a few moves have been made, we find White mourning his lost initiative as he finds himself on the defensive.

KING FIANCHETTO

WHITE	BLACK
1 P—KN3	P—K4

Now Black intends to answer 2 B—N2 with 2 ... P—Q4 with a magnificent Pawn center. So White abjectly changes his mind after all.

2 P—Q4	PxP	3 QxP	N—QB3!

White's unprepared thrust in the center has enabled Black to gain time for development.

4 Q—QR4	B—B4	7 P—B3	B—Q2
5 B—N2	KN—K2	8 Q—B2	B—B4!
6 N—KB3	P—Q3	9 P—K4	B—Q2

Black has provoked P—K4 in order to induce White to block the diagonal of his fianchettoed Bishop. As matters stand, Black is already ahead in development and can face the future with confidence.

10 QN—Q2	Q—B1	13 N—B4	P—Q4
11 P—KR3	Castles	14 NxB	BPxN!
12 P—QN4?	B—N3		

115

Black will exert lasting pressure along the Queen Bishop file.

White has weakened his position badly with 12 P—QN4? as part of a maneuver to deprive Black of the two Bishops. Black's unexpected recapture (instead of the normal 14 . . . RPxN) has opened the Queen Bishop file for Black, enabling him to operate against White's permanently weakened Queen Bishop Pawn. Thus Black has obtained a clear positional advantage.

| 15 B—QR3 | PxP | 16 N—N5 | N—Q5! |

Black parries the threat of P—N5 and at the same time prepares simplifying exchanges that will set off his advantage.

| 17 Q—Q2 | N—B6ch | 18 BxN | .... |

Or 18 NxN, PxN; 19 BxP, BxP; 20 BxP?, QxB; 21 RxB, Q—N7 and Black wins a Rook.

| 18 .... | PxB | 20 Q—Q3 | N—N3 |
| 19 Castles(Q) | B—R5 | 21 R—Q2 | B—N4! |

For after 22 QxB, QxPch; 23 K—Q1, QxB Black wins easily. And 22 QxP?, B—B3 is even worse for White.

22 Q—B2	B—K7!	25 RxRch	QxR
23 P—R4	P—B4	26 QxP	Q—B3
24 P—N5	R—Q1	27 QxQ	....

Equally hopeless for White is 27 Q—B2, BxP, etc.

27	PxQ	30 K—Q2	R—Q1!
28 N—K4	K—N2	31 K—K3	N—N5ch!
29 N—Q6	N—K4		

This is even quicker than 31 . . . RxN; 32 BxR, N—B5ch and 33 . . . NxB; for now Black's advanced King Bishop Pawn becomes a passed Pawn.

| 32 K—B4 | NxP | | 34 N—B5ch | K—B2 |
| 33 R—QN1 | N—N5 | | Resigns | |

White is helpless; for example, 35 N—K3, P—B7; 36 N—B1, R—Q8; 37 RxR, BxR and the coming 38 . . . B—K7 wins a piece.

In this exceedingly instructive game, Black's relentlessly logical play exacted the full penalty for White's slipshod opening lapses.

The Queen Fianchetto

As we shall see in the following game, 1 P—QN3 is an equally unfavorable way to start the game. Once more Black has a free hand in the center and an unhampered development. It therefore comes as no surprise that Black quickly seizes the initiative and carries out a powerful and even brilliant sacrificial attack. The following game is a good example of the consequences of such an opening.

QUEEN FIANCHETTO

WHITE	BLACK		WHITE	BLACK
1 P—QN3	P—Q4		4 N—KB3	B—N2
2 B—N2	N—KB3		5 P—KR3	Castles
3 P—K3	P—KN3		6 P—KN4?	. . . .

Once more we repeat the story of the previous game. Black has been allowed to develop comfortably, under no pressure and with no defensive problems. White therefore makes an attacking gesture which is intended to terrify Black. Instead, the intended attacking move merely weakens White's game, while Black, profoundly unimpressed, calmly continues his development.

| 6 . . . . | P—B4 | | 8 P—Q3 | B—Q2 |
| 7 B—N2 | N—B3 | | 9 QN—Q2 | Q—B2 |

Black is building up an ideal development, with a view to an eventual . . . P—K4 and an overwhelming position in the center.

| 10 N—B1 | KR—Q1 | 11 N—N3? | NxP! |

A neat combination made possible by Black's excellent development. The point is that after 12 BxB there follows 12 . . . NxKP! and Black is two Pawns to the good.

| 12 PxN | BxB | 14 N—Q2 | N—K4 |
| 13 QR—N1 | B—B6ch | 15 B—B3 | .... |

White cannot defend his King Knight Pawn with 15 P—B3, for then 15 . . . NxQPch! wins another Pawn.

| 15 .... | Q—R4 |

Black threatens to win a piece by 16 . . . BxNch or 16 . . . NxBch. White has been completely outplayed, and Black has the whip hand.

| 16 N/N3—B1 | QxP |

Now Black threatens 17 . . . NxBch; 18 QxN, QxRch.

| 17 B—K2 | Q—R4 |

Also possible was 17 . . . BxP, but Black is content.

| 18 P—B4 | N—B3 | 20 B—B3 | P—Q5! |
| 19 K—B2 | Q—B2! | 21 N—K4 | PxPch |

If now 22 KxP, . . . B—Q5ch wins easily.

| 22 K—N3 | B—N2 | 23 NxKP | B—K1 |

Indirectly guarding his Queen Bishop Pawn, for if 24 NxP?, B—Q5 wins.

24 Q—KB1   P—KR3!   25 P—B3?   ....

White falls into a subtle trap.

116

Black has a brilliant Queen sacrifice.

25 ....   QxPch!!

For if 26 KxQ, B—K4 mate.

26 K—B2   N—K4

White resigns, as Black must win more material.

An ideal refutation of White's faulty opening. Black carefully and skillfully built up an overwhelming position and took perfectly timed advantage of White's shortcomings.

Faulty play after 1 P—K4

In the two previous games we have seen how quickly White can forfeit the initiative by playing unusual openings which neglect development and ignore the problem of controlling the center.

It is true that after 1 P—K4 White has far better prospects than in these irregular openings. But even after 1 P—K4 White can go wrong and thereby nullify all the benefits he should have from playing this excellent first move. For example:

IRREGULAR OPENING

WHITE	BLACK	WHITE	BLACK
1 P—K4	P—K4	2 B—K2	....

A queer move. White exerts no pressure on Black's game (as he would with 2 N—KB3). At the same time he deprives himself of the possibility of later developing the Bishop more aggressively, say to Queen Bishop 4 or Queen Knight 5.

2	N—KB3	3 P—Q3	N—B3

The players have changed roles. White has voluntarily assumed the defensive, and Black has an easy development. Just one harmless-looking move—White's colorless 2 B—K2 —makes all the difference.

4 N—QB3	B—N5	7 B—N5	P—KR3
5 N—B3	P—Q3	8 B—Q2	N—K2
6 Castles	Castles	9 Q—B1	....

Very significant. Because of the puny development ushered in by 2 B—K2, White has no good square for his Queen. Meanwhile Black plays to obtain more mobility for his pieces by opening the King Bishop file.

9	N—R2	11 KPxP	....
10 P—Q4	P—KB4		

The alternative 11 QPxP, BxN; 12 BxB, BPxP; 13 N—Q2, P—Q4 does not offer much scope to the White Bishops.

11	BxN	14 NxN	BxN
12 BxB	P—K5	15 P—Q5	Q—R5
13 N—R4	NxP	16 P—B3	....

White has worked conscientiously at the job of freeing his game, and here 16 Q—K3 would be more to the point, although Black would still have the initiative.

| 16 .... | QR—K1! | 18 Q—Q2 | .... |
| 17 PxP | BxP | | |

For one brief moment it seems as if White has worked his way out of his troubles, as he now intends to exchange Rooks on the open King Bishop file or dispute its control. But Black is now prepared to assert brusquely that the superior placement of his pieces does matter after all.

117

Black has a clever tactical finesse.

18 ....   BxNP!

The point is that if 19 KxB, Q—N4ch! and Black has an easy endgame win after 20 QxQ, RxBch or 20 K—R1, QxQ; 21 BxQ, RxB.

| 19 RxRch | RxR | 20 B—Q3 | .... |

Of course not 20 KxB?, R—B7ch and mate next move.

20 ....   B—R6

White resigns. Why?

Black threatens . . . N—N4 followed by . . . N—B6ch with decisive effect. White must play 21 BxNch, but after 21 . . . KxB; 22 Q—Q3ch, B—B4; 23 Q—Q2, B—K5! White is helpless against the coming . . . Q—N5ch—unless he prefers to lose a second Pawn with 24 Q—K1, Q—N5ch!; 25 Q—N3, QxQch; 26 PxQ, BxQP. This would leave Black with an easy win, so White prefers to give up the struggle at once.

The three examples in this chapter show convincingly that the search for "exotic" openings can only harm White and benefit Black. The violation of sound opening principles leads in each case to a fine development and a comfortable initiative for Black. Consequently there is every reason why Black should welcome these bizarre experiments on White's part.

INDEX